A NEW DESIGN FOR FAMILY MINISTRY

Dr. Dennis B. Guernsey

David C. Cook Publishing Co.
Elgin, Illinois—Weston, Ontario

A NEW DESIGN FOR FAMILY MINISTRY

© 1982 Dennis B. Guernsey

Third Printing January, 1988

Published by David C. Cook Publishing Co.
850 N. Grove Ave., Elgin, IL 60120
Edited by Dave and Neta Jackson
Cover design by Douglas Norrgard
Printed in the United States of America
Library of Congress Catalog Number: 82-72793
ISBN: 0-89191-650-4

For those friends who have become our "family of families": Skip and Ann, Ron and Barbie, Paul and Jan, Dale and Marilyn, Wayne and Nancy, Scott and Diane.

Contents

Contents

1 Confused Loyalties

Few would disagree that there is a growing, even overwhelming, interest in matters having to do with the family, especially among those of us who are Christian. What was once a distant cry, the anguish of broken and breaking families, is now a present and constant roar. Hardly anyone in the Evangelical subculture has been untouched. Friends, family, and we ourselves, have felt the hurt of strained and fractured relationships. Statistics having to do with marital dissolution, runaways, increase in major crimes, and other seemingly relevant data fill the books we read and the sermons we hear. The alarm has gone out. We are getting the message. But what is to be our response? We cannot be passive. Something must be done, but what?

It is my opinion that much of what is being done, the frantic bleating of statistics and doom, is counterproductive. Our panic adds to the fear already experienced by those who are hurting from the battle.

I am reminded of the statistics having to do with "body counts" during the Vietnam war. The more the numbers were chanted by those who were responsible for administering the war, the greater became our callousness to the numbers and eventually they lost their significance. The steady reminder of the events soon diminished their importance to us.

It is time to move beyond the fear and rage toward a positive and hopeful program of both remediation and prevention. To keep on yelling "fire" when all have been alarmed, is to contribute to the tenuousness and unsteadiness of those needing help. To promote panic is not the answer. What shall we do? Let me approach the issue in another way. I have asked a number of gifted, successful, respected pastors and education specialists, "Why do you think your church should minister to and strengthen its families?" The answers represent a wide continuum but seem to fall into at least three categories.

First, there are those who minister to families because it's part of the role they have been trained to play, part of their function as a pastor or associate. It is what they "do" even if the reasons are forgotten or unclear. Of the three, this answer seems to be the most superficial. It is function without purpose, activity

1

without practical or theoretical integration.

The second reason for ministering to families in the local church is articulated as follows: Families are people; people are hurting; and people are important. The difference between this reason and the first one is its focus. The first focuses upon function and the second focuses upon people. Pastors are to be "people helpers," encouragers, confronters, etc. My observation is that those who hold this as their basic reason for ministering to families are more people oriented and less program oriented. Their theology is more relational and less dogmatic. Their lack, however, is in their inability to conceptualize the difference between the individual and the family, between the part and the whole. They are able to articulate their reasons for reaching individuals for Christ, but are unable to articulate the reasons for preserving and protecting the families from which those individuals come. Most often, the family or marriage orientation of those who hold to this position is a corrective orientation. They are regularly involved with counseling the marriages and the families in their church who are hurting. As a result, they are deeply aware of others' pain. The people of God are hurting, and they share their hurt.

The third reason given for ministering to families goes one step beyond the previous two, and the step is both logical and theological. Families are important because they were created by God and whatever God has touched is important. Somewhere in the distant past is the memory of a course in theology in which the Creation narratives of the Book of Genesis are remembered and the theological implications of those narratives linger. Something about the husband and wife relationship mirrors the Godhead and is essential to a concept of the Trinity (Barth, 1956; Brunner, 1962; Bonhoeffer, 1971), but that's about as far as it goes—vague and distant memories. The integrity of the family is thus maintained but the implications in terms of the New Testament are left untouched. The activities have reasons, and the reasons are theological, but they are primitive.

It was just such "primitive" reasoning that proved to be the catalyst for this book. I had been invited as an outside consultant to an elders' retreat for a thriving local church. Although the director of Christian education had been the one to arrange for my coming, the key person for the church and for the weekend was the senior pastor. He was a man known for his ability and for his commitment, and I was pleased to be invited and looked forward to the experience. When the weekend arrived, the pastor was obviously in control. He had the respect of his board of elders, and from the way they were organized, it was obvious that much planning and preparation had gone into the retreat. My role was to be a resource person and a provocateur. I was to be an ombudsman for the families in their church.

For eight hours, on Saturday we probed and discussed their philosophy of ministry, especially as it related to my field of expertise, the family. I was thoroughly impressed. The questions of both the staff and the board were relevant and direct. Their evaluations of what they were doing were blunt and to the point. More than once, they squirmed under the penetrating light of the discussion. When the weekend was over, I had a gut feeling that they would come down off that mountain with a prioritized agenda for their church, one that would result in a better ecology for the families of that church.

The board had shared both individually and collectively that they, too, were hurting. They were feeling the stress and strain of taut marriages, rebellious teenagers, and rebellion within themselves in the form of fantasies, lusts, and misadventures. The problem of the disintegration of the family was not "out there." It was a part of who they were. Their island fortress, the church, had been breached, not by heresy, not by division or strife, but by the quiet, silent erosion of relationships. No one in the room was exempt. We had revealed ourselves to be both persecutors and victims. When the weekend was finished, I was sure their concerns would carry over into their programs throughout the year.

As I gathered my luggage together, the senior pastor called my name and asked if he could walk me to my car. He was genuinely friendly, warm, and gregarious—the model of a successful pastor. I had heard him that day make himself vulnerable, and the response of his board was deeply appreciative.

"It's been a good day, hasn't it? But there's one thing that is still bothering me. I just can't seem to get beyond it. Frankly, we were all around it but never hit it hard."

I was curious. It seemed to me that we had dealt with the bottom line head-on. But he was obviously provoked and agitated, if only just under the surface. I decided to let him finish his agenda.

"Dennis. Why is there such an emphasis and concern about the family? Oh, I know people are hurting, but they've been hurting since the Creation and the Fall. What's of greater importance to me is God's institution, the Church."

I couldn't believe my ears. I was crushed.

As he benevolently walked me to my car with his arm around my shoulder, our conversation continued but I don't remember what was said beyond his opening statement. I had a sinking feeling in the pit of my stomach. Our eight hours together had penetrated only superficially. He was still at ground zero regarding the family, and I was awash in frustration.

I thought I had made my point. I had assumed that I had established the need for the leadership to respond to the needs of the institution of the family as well as the needs of the Church. I had said, although I must admit it was in passing, that both the family and the Church had been created by God. Both were valid. Both were necessary. He had listened, but he had not heard.

My first response was to become aggressive, to prove him wrong. But I backed off from my initial inclination. Nothing could be done at that time. I thanked him for the opportunity to be with him and left.

Later, on the long drive down the mountain in the car alone, I had to admit that the fault was not his. The fault was mine. I had been presumptuous. I had assumed that a man who was deeply committed to Christ and to the building of Christ's Kingdom would be as equally committed to the families of those who made up that Kingdom. To my chagrin I had focused on the wrong target. However valid my motives and however urgent the needs of that flock, this open and dear man of God had not bridged the relationship between the Church and the family.

4

Unconsciously in his mind the Church was God's institution and the family was tangential, supplemental to the growth of the Church.

I was sure that if I asked him directly if he believed that the needs of the families of his church were secondary to the needs of his church, I would evoke a strong denial. But, likewise, if I were to ask him to articulate the interrelationship between the Church and the family, he would stumble and struggle for answers. Although he had probably preached numerous sermons on family-related topics, he had never thought through the place of the family as an institution in the building of the Kingdom of God. On that he was utterly naive.

My experience that day provoked me to ask how many other assumptions I had been making, assumptions that were eroding my ability to articulate the urgency I felt about the family. Further reflection led me to realize that I had made three such assumptions.

In the first place, I had assumed that a leader's commitment to the church automatically implied a commitment to the families of that church. Latent within that assumption is the notion that the leadership of the Church understands the interrelationship between the Church and the family. I have since come to realize that such is not the case. In fact, we have done very little to articulate the issues. If the water is muddy, the swimmers cannot be faulted if they cannot see the bottom. Part of the reason for this book is to facilitate a dialogue about the interrelationship between the Church and the family.

The second assumption has to do with the methodology of a ministry to the family. It is the other side of the coin from the first assumption. I had assumed that a philosophy and methodology of ministry designed to support and expand the ministry of the Church would automatically support an expanded ministry to the family as well. We cannot assume that the educational philosophy of the Church will be supportive of the families in the Church. How can this be so?

The answer lies in the difference between education and socialization, between instruction and nurture. For the most part the educational function of the church has been influenced by

5

philosophies of public education. The result has been the notion that the family is outmoded in its ability to educate its young. The functions that once belonged to the family have now been distributed among other institutions which supposedly can do the job better. Unfortunately the church has tacitly agreed. While giving lip service to the integrity of the family, we continue to create and deliver programs that compete with the family.

I have come to believe that the task of the family is identical to that of the Church. Our tasks include socialization and nurture. It is our identical tasks that make us coequal in the Kingdom of God.

The third, and perhaps the most debilitating assumption is the one concerning the state of the art of marriage and family ministry. It is a fact that for all *practical* and effective purposes neither a theology nor a methodology of marriage and family ministry now exists. What does exist is the popularization of both ancient and contemporary psychological and sociological models, none of which is necessarily Christian. While it is true that these models *might be* consistent with Scripture, the rampant and indiscriminate application of secular models at the popular level in many ways has led us down our present path. Said in another way, the plethora of books about the family and family-related topics at the popular level has not provided us with solid theological footings upon which to build a methodology of ministry to the family. We have built our house from the attic downward, paying too little attention to the importance of the foundations.

Most categories of theology, whether systematic or Biblical, have hundreds of years of history behind them. Great doctrines of the Church have evolved through the push and the pull of rigorous dialogue. Councils, confessions, and creeds have articulated the subtle hues of those doctrines. Likewise, God has raised up great people with outstanding intellect to sharpen the issues. But what about a theology of the family? A recent examination of the theological literature identified less than 250 pages of substantive theology about the family. That's not much in almost 2,000 years of history. Why?

It is informative, I think, that the interest in the family has been provoked by the cries of the people. Those who are seeking to bring order to the chaos are simply trying to keep up with the problems. The analogy of the first-century church comes to mind. On that occasion plain, sometimes ignorant leaders were trying to bring order out of the chaos of thousands of converts to Christianity, often in the tumult of persecution, the dislocation of families, and the emergence out of heathen background. Much of the New Testament was given in response to the cries of God's people. If it had not been for the guidance of the Holy Spirit, the task would have been hopeless. Theology often flows out of ministry which in turn flows out of need, and not vice versa. If this was true in the beginning of the Church, it is true even now. Bookstores are stocked with books about the family because that is where the pain is. My purpose is not to denigrate those books. Instead, I only mean to draw attention to the fact that both a theology of the family and a subsequent methodology is at best infant.

We must be careful as to what we say about the family as well as tolerant about our differences. We cannot expect our efforts to be fully orbed, totally consistent, and polished in the sense that other issues in theology are. To say that we have no answers would be wrong. However, I am afraid that we err at the other extreme. We often represent our family-related books, sermons, or ideas, to be a cure-all, end-all answer to the questions that are being asked. The issues facing the family are far too complicated to be handled so quickly and so superficially. I shudder at the so-called "truths" that are broadcast as if they have been proven to be absolute, Biblical authority. The state of the art should caution us to speak with growing confidence but certainly not with dogmatism.

As a beginning point I would suggest two areas in which much work needs to be done.

Establish Rules of Interpretation

To begin with, much work needs to be done in the formulation of a hermeneutic to be used in interpreting Biblical material relating to the family. To say it in another way, the rules for interpreting the Bible, when applied to family themes, must be carefully and thoughtfully established. For example, how is it that some Christians interpret the apostle Paul's teaching regarding the authority of men over women in I Corinthians 11 to be universal while at the same time take his teaching in the same chapter regarding hair and the covering of the head to be culturally specific, that is, particular to that day and age. Similar inconsistencies are common. The answers are not easy and much work needs to be done especially by those of us who hold the Word of God to be the ultimate authority for our lives.

Acknowledge Our Cultural Blinders

Secondly, we need to be open to the very real intrusion of our cultural perspective into our Biblical interpretation and application. Most thoughtful scholars agree that the family is the cradle of any culture and that the perceptions of the culture are those of its families. It is a kind of hand-in-glove phenomenon. Each is cause and each is effect for the other. At no other place and in no other subspeciality of theology will culture be more intrusive than in those areas affecting the family. As a result, the very real probability of misinterpretation exists. Our own culture is like the air we breathe. Our lungs expand and contract thousands of times daily without a purposive thought. We do not will ourselves to draw breath. The air is just "there." So it is in the way we perceive the family. All families should be like the family our culture holds up to be the ideal. Any other is to be thought of as deviant. Other points of view are to be shunned as wrong.

As interpreters of Scripture our hard task is to sort out the contamination of our own culture from the Biblical and also to find the interrelationships between the two.

Such is the *raison d'être* for this book. It is written for the purpose of entering the serious dialogue about the philosophy and methodology of family ministry. I make no great and inclusive truth claims about what is said. I do assert that I have been processing the material in my own life and ministry for over 15 years. I fully recognize that it is only a beginning. I encourage you to join in the journey as well.

Does the Church Need Its Families?

2

The place to begin in the formulation of an answer to this very important question is with our ultimate authority, Jesus Himself, and His Word, the Scriptures. As simplistic as this may seem on the surface, I don't think that we have yet made the connection between the commands of Jesus upon our lives (and thus upon the Church) and the viability of the family as an institution. It's just that connection or interrelationship that I believe to be a kind of linchpin for a ministry to families. For those of us who seek to serve Christ and His Church, it is where we must begin.

Of the many passages in the New Testament where one could begin to formulate a philosophy of ministry to the family, I would like to suggest the Great Commission found in Matthew's Gospel, chapter 28:

> Go therefore and make disciples of all nations, bap-
> tizing them in the name of the Father and of the Son
> and of the Holy Spirit, teaching them to observe all
> that I have commanded you; and lo, I am with you
> always, to the close of the age (Mt. 28:19-20, RSV).

The importance of this message by Christ to His disciples has been well established in the theological literature (Ladd, 1974).

What I would like to do in this chapter is to look at Christ's Great Commission, not through the eyes of the theologian or exegete, but through the eyes of the family sociologist. I would suggest that the ministry imperatives for the Church are found in this passage, and these imperatives are critically interrelated with a ministry to the families of our churches. I believe the three directives of the passage highlight the importance of a family to the Church.

Families Make or Break Disciples

Jesus said that the Church is to "Go therefore, and make disciples of all nations." The critical question is, what is a disciple? A commonly accepted definition would be that from Rengstorf. A disciple is one who has formed a personal allegiance to Jesus and has committed himself to learn of Him (Rengstorf,

1967). Such definitions major on the function or the character of the disciple. From another perspective, that of the family sociologist, the focus might be placed upon the nature of the relationship between the disciple and his teacher. To state it in sociological terms, a disciple is one who has entered into a close, *primary relationship* with the one who has become his teacher. The concept of a "primary relationship" was set forth by Charles H. Cooley in the late 1920's. Groups could be classified as either primary or secondary, according to Cooley (1929). A primary group is any small, intimate group that is especially important to the individual as a source of emotional satisfaction. On the other hand, a secondary group is distinguished by the fact that it is relatively impersonal although it is not necessarily "secondary" in terms of its effects on the individual's life. Primary relationships are characterized by intimacy as opposed to function, by their personal nature rather than the impersonal, and by their sensitivity rather than insensitivity.

For purposes of our discussion, a "family" is taken to mean that primary group from which the individual derives his or her earliest sense of belonging or identity. It most commonly consists of the husband-wife and/or parent-child relationships, although it can include others in the extended family, or household, who relate intimately with the individual. Thus, it may include the nuclear family, the extended family, the single-parent family, etc. (Goldberg and Deutsch, 1977.)

The questions that are central to my thesis are where are primary relationships formed, and where are the skills for forming such relationships learned? The relationships are formed and the skills are learned within the context of primary groups (Cooley, 1922). To diminish the effectiveness of the primary group is to diminish the effectiveness of the relationship as well as diminish the skills for forming other primary relationships (Parsons and Bales, 1955).

And which primary group is central to the first learning of these skills? They are learned for better or for worse in the family (Mussen, et. al., 1979). Through the processes of attachment and interaction children learn to associate intimately with their caretakers to the degree they have interrelated with them (Har-

10

low and Harlow, 1966). The family becomes that first laboratory in which the child practices his skills of relationship as well as develops his sense of self-esteem and/or self-concept (Mead, 1934; Cooley, 1922; Sullivan, 1953).

Thus, the logic of the equation is formed. If disciples are those who relate with their teacher in the context of a primary relationship, then the *capacity* to form primary relationships is necessary to the process of disciple making. Secondly, if primary relationships consist of relationship skills that are generalized from one primary group to another, then the family is key in its significance because it is the place where those skills are learned well or learned poorly. And last of all, if the family is the social organization in which these skills are learned first, and thus most essentially, then the family becomes central to the process of disciple making. It is a place where disciplelike relational skills are learned, and it is a primary group in which disciple making takes place.

To say it in a practical way, in the context of my relationship as parent to my child, two processes are taking place: I am either discipling or not discipling my child for Christ's sake, and I am teaching my child to relate either primarily or secondarily to me and to others. Because of our natural processes of attachment and interaction no one can accomplish these two functions better than I can. If I fail, someone else must compensate for my failure. If I succeed, the discipling process has been most efficiently served and Christ's directive is fulfilled in part.

In terms of the Great Commission, the implications for the Church are enormous. As a leader in the Church, it only makes sense that I ally myself with that primary group who can do the job of disciple making most naturally and efficiently, that is, the family. To spend my time otherwise just doesn't make sense.

But in reality, as leaders of the Church, we spend a great deal of our time trying to create new primary groups where there are none (such as in Sunday school classes, youth groups, small groups, etc.) while at the same time failing to nurture, stimulate and protect that primary group where the potential of disciple-making is going on every day and every night of the week. In truth, families make or break disciples, and in the process the

11

task of the Church is made easier or more difficult.

Families Are "Baptizers"

The second directive for ministry in the Great Commission is to baptize these disciples in the name of the Father, the Son, and the Holy Spirit. The differences in the Church over the mode of baptism is not central to the present discussion. What is central is the meaning of baptism as it was experienced by those in the first-century church. Baptism was that event in which the individual identified himself with Jesus as Jesus has redemptively identified Himself with mankind. The essential process of identification with the risen Christ was and is inherent to the meaning of baptism (Oepke, 1964). Again, as in the case of disciple making, I would like to approach this issue from the point of view of a family sociologist.

One way to conceptualize the phenomenon of baptism and its inherent meaning of identification is to view it from the perspective of socialization. Socialization refers to the process by which persons acquire the knowledge, skills, and dispositions that make them more or less able members of their society (Brim, 1966; Goslin, 1969). Socialization is the process through which a given culture builds into its fledgling members the role expectations and status that are important to that culture. It is the process by which any group or subculture translates those who are "out there" into those who are "one of us," the journey from "they" to "we." What I am suggesting is that Jesus has instructed us through the symbolism of baptism to bring those who are "out there" to "in here," the process of becoming "fellowcitizens" and "no more strangers and foreigners" from the family of God (Eph. 2:19).

How does that happen? How can we compel those who are converted to become identified with Him? How can we most efficiently move beyond the symbol to the meaning behind the event?

The answer to our question is critical in terms of the mission of the Church. Baptism, irrespective of your interpretation of the event, is more than a hollow symbol. It is the beginning of a

12

process, and the process is that of socialization into the Christian community. Socialization involves not only the communication of information but also the building in of the skills and motivations necessary to fulfill the demands incurred by the new expectations in the person's life. Socialization is therefore a more inclusive term. It is the bringing of a fledgling member to a place of maturity in the group. Socialization is therefore more than education. It is the "fitting in" of the person into his or her place. Baptism, from the point of view of the family sociologist, becomes that act of identification which begins the process of socialization, a process that is finished only when the person is brought to maturity in Christ.

The question that naturally follows is, who can best bring that person to maturity in Christ? For centuries the task has fallen to the family to be the prime agent of socialization into broader society. Only since the 1930's has the socialization function of the family been in question. Unfortunately, the Church has fallen into the trap of becoming shaped by the spirit of the age. I'm sure without malice, the family has been ignored by the church leaders as the primary agent of socialization of children into their place in the Church. We have been brought to believe that families are inadequate to the task. Therefore, we set about creating new groups and organizations to socialize the fledgling members. We are guilty of reinventing the wheel every time we create or build a group to function in the place of the primary group that already exists, the family.

But another question immediately surfaces: What about those people whose natural families are bereaved of any spiritual interest or direction? Are we not responsible for them? My answer is a strong "yes!" But what we must understand is that to minister effectively to those without viable Christian families we must build new family structures for them. Socialization takes place best in the compelling structure of a family, whether that family be natural or surrogate. In this case we are repairing rather than reinventing the wheel.

Today, in the Western world, a high percentage of people now needing evangelizing come from families which in some generation of the past were strongly and soundly Christian. If those families had been encouraged, taught, and supported by the Church to do their internal discipling and "baptizing" (socializing) effectively, the Great Commission would have been much more nearly fulfilled today. To neglect the family as the Church's first priority for fulfilling the Great Commission is to make its fulfillment much harder in the future.

The upshot of my argument is that the Church is in the "family" business, whether that involves the strengthening of viable, existing family units, or the creating of new centers of nurture for those who are in need of Christian nurture.

When we, as leaders of the Church become supportive of this function, we are completing the task of socialization, the task that undergirds the symbol.

Families Build in Values

The third, and last, directive from Christ in the Great Commission is to teach those whom we have discipled to obey everything He has commanded us to do. From the perspective of the family sociologist, the phenomenon of obedience to Christ might be cast in terms of the acquisition of a value system similar to that of Christ's. This would be the emphasis of writers in the area of Biblical theology such as Ladd and others (Ladd, 1974; Berkouwer, 1962). Values can be defined as that system of priorities one assigns to the objects, both material and immaterial, in one's world (Sager, 1976). The capacity to assign priorities follows closely with the capacity of language and the assignment of symbols to the phenomenal world. It is that function of socialization referred to by Jones and Gerard as "information dependence and cognitive socialization" (Jones and Gerard, 1967). Whatever the process children follow in the acquisition of language, the end result is that they order their world in much the same way as those from whom they learn to speak (Brown, 1973). Language is the bearer of culture and through the acquisition of language the older generation passes on the structures that are deemed important to the younger generation (Lindesmith and Strauss, 1968).

Building a Christian value system happens similarly to the

14

process of disciple making and socialization. It is the *family* that most normally presents the child with the capacity of language, and it is the *family* that passes on its culture and value system through the vehicle of that language.

I am of the opinion that Jesus Christ was crucified by His antagonists in the main because of the clash between His value system and theirs. (Cf. Mt. 15:1-20.) He dared to break with the traditions of the elders. He ran contrary to the dominant culture of His day, that of the scribes and the Pharisees.

Similarly, in our day I am of the opinion that the battleground between the god of this world and the Lord of the Universe is the arena of the prevailing value system of God's people. It is for this reason that we are to be renewed in our mind (Rom. 12:2). We are to adopt as our own that system of priorities that characterized Jesus of Nazareth in both His attitudes and behaviors. We are not to be "conformed to this world: but . . . transformed" and thus fulfill God's will for us (Rom. 12:2).

By now my intent is obvious. Obedience in terms of both how to be obedient and what it is we are to do so as to obey is either learned or not learned in the boundaries of our first primary group, the family. To whatever degree a Christian family succeeds in passing on the value system espoused by Jesus, that is the degree to which the process of obedience to His commands is achieved, apart from remedial help. As the giver of language and as the bearer of culture, no other institution can do the job more efficiently. Wise is the person who joins hands with those who can do the job best.

Conclusion

My central thesis has been to establish the mutual interdependence between the major task of the Church—the fulfillment of the Great Commission—and the natural tasks of the family. I recommend a model for ministry that parallels the Church's tasks of making disciples, baptism, and teaching obedience, with the family tasks of establishing primary relationships, socialization, and building values. It is a healthy symbiosis (two dissimilar groups in a mutually beneficial relationship) between the Church and the family, an interdependence that mandates a ministry to families by the Church.

I contend that the importance of the family to the Church is much more than we realize and that the present attack upon the integrity of the family as an institution may well be the enemy's most pointed attack upon the Church. But when the Church strengthens its families, it allies itself with its families in such a way so as to effectively fulfill its own purpose for being, the fulfillment of the Great Commission.

3
Some Churches Help; Others Hinder

When I was in seminary, I worked as a probation officer for the juvenile court. My duties involved night intake. I was the officer of the court that often had to decide whether or not to return an erring juvenile to his or her parents or to detain the kid until the next day. Also, I often had to decide what to do with younger, dependent children, who, *through no fault of their own,* had come into the custody of the police because of their parents' neglect or their parents' arrest. The four and a half years I worked for the juvenile department was an education of another type.

Many parents were blatantly remiss in their task of parenting, and mournfully admitted their failures with their children. But I never once had a parent admit that he or she had *intended* to do a lousy job. Their hearts were always in the right place. But the bottom line, their behavior, was someplace else.

This illustration demonstrates that it is possible for one's intent to be inconsistent with one's behavior. In particular, I'm concerned about the consistency of church leaders toward the family. I'm convinced that nowhere in the world today would you find a pastor or a director of Christian education who would admit to intentionally programming against the interests of the family or to making decisions that consciously hinder Christian family living. Out there, in the educational establishment of Christian higher learning, I doubt if we could find a lecture entitled, "How to Foul Up the Families of Your Church."

On the other hand, I wonder if we are ready to lay claim to the opposite: that none of our decisions, none of our programs, and none of our lectures have had a negative effect upon the families who constitute our flock. I think not. Somewhere inside our organizational consciences, we sense that we, too, have erred. How difficult it is to take that cold, hard, objective look at ourselves and become our own critics. It is all too easy to defend our blind spots because somehow our "motives" have been good. Unfortunately, I'm afraid that too many of us are just like those parents at the juvenile department. The fruits of our mismanagement are being laid at our doorsteps, but the purity of our intentions leads us to rationalize our culpability.

However, I have faith that, when faced with the facts, we can and will accept the responsibility. The buck *does* stop with us. So, we must ask ourselves, are we making it better or are we making it worse for families? The answer for each church will probably fall somewhere on a continuum which I'll try to describe by identifying four points on the continuum.

The Parasitic Church

On the most negative side of the continuum is the parasitic church. A parasite is defined as that organism, or in this case organization, that feeds off its host without making constructive or positive contribution to that host. Parasites are legion throughout nature. Even the word has come to elicit a flesh-crawling response when we hear it mentioned. But how can a church be a parasite? Let me suggest several ways.

In the first place, a church might be considered parasitic in terms of the way it relates to its professional staff. Does the church think of its pastor and staff wholly in terms of itself without reference to the family of that pastor? Do the members of the church have unbridled access to the leadership without thinking of the families of the leadership? Are the pastor or the elders expected to lead even though the pay or the remuneration is inadequate? Are we paying for the privilege of meeting together as a church out of the financial hide of the leadership? Let me give you an example.

I know of a very doctrinally sound local church that hangs on to its own existence by asking its pastor year after year to forgo even a cost-of-living raise. Even though the church serves a middle- to upper-middle-class congregation, the pastor is asked to live with a yearly wage near that of the poverty level. When the pastor finally gathered up enough courage to ask the church board for a raise, they had the temerity to ask him to submit a detailed budget demonstrating how he was spending his money. When the pastor challenged them about their request, their retort was to classify him in a different category from themselves. He was expected ''to serve in humility.'' When he pushed them further, they all agreed that personally they would

18

never submit what they were asking of him in their own places of employment. When the pastor persisted (by now he had become angry), they each wrote on a secret ballot their yearly salary, only to find out that their average was more than twice that of their pastor. Clearly the church was not paying their pastor the honor he deserved, and that is the nature of a parasite.

Another characteristic of the parasitic church might be how it views its mission. There are only three commodities that we humans have with which to transact life: space, time, and energy. The church becomes parasitic when it consistently preempts the family in any one of these three areas.

Space has reference to geography. Our tendency, at least in the American church, is to define the church in terms of its geographic location—a place, a building. The extreme of such a mind-set is to assume that the place is automatically more important than the people. The church building is treated as if it were the center of the universe. Life begins and ends there. It is like the medieval church smugly set atop a hill, and the peasants are expected to arrange their lives and their homes about it. To be parasitic in terms of space is to unconsciously assume that the church as *place* should be the center of the people's world.

The second commodity is that of time. Time involves the hours of the day and the months of the year. In the illustration I mentioned above, the church was parasitic in that the members of the church related to their pastor as if he or his family had no right to a clock or a calendar of their own. They wanted complete and absolute access.

On the other hand, it is often the pastoral leadership of a church that is guilty of just such thinking toward the people of the church. For example, take a look at the time and number of regularly scheduled meetings. I have known of pastors who demanded, however gently, that meetings be held only during prime time, prime not in terms of television but in terms of the family's opportunity to be together. The reason given is that you're more likely to be able to "get them there." Such an attitude is parasitic in its rawest form. It falsely requires the people to make a choice between the church and the family, assuming that the church schedule should be given first priority in terms of the hours of the day or the months of the year.

The third commodity is that of energy. That is, what we *do* with our time. In terms of the parasitic church, the energy demands are seemingly limitless. One residual effect of such demands is mid-life dropout.

I recently had the occasion to have a discussion with a small group of committed Christian laymen. The essence of the discussion focused upon the demands made upon them by their church, a church they all seemed to love. Without exception they complained of severe fatigue and wondered what they could do about it. Each of the men had served through the years on the ruling boards of the church, only now to find themselves functioning on the periphery of church life with little motivation to reenter the demands of leadership. They found it difficult to attend all of the regular services of the church. They resisted being appointed to any position of responsibility. Without exception, they were looking forward to weekends away from the church, whether in a camper, at a cabin, or just "away from it all." The general tenor of their conversation was unanimous fatigue. They were dropouts.

Later, I was asked by their pastor to spend some time with him consulting about his recent rash of resignations. He was running out of leaders, and he was searching for the reasons. As he and I talked, I became aware of his total single-mindedness. All that was important to him was his church. It was as if nothing else existed but the local institution. He could not understand that others couldn't match, or even chose not to match, his absolute commitment to it. As I listened I noticed a curious twist in his perceptions. Commitment to his church, measured in terms of the space, time, and energy, was coequal with commitment to Christ. To be less committed than he, was to be uncommitted to Christ. To him what was good for his church was obviously God's will, the thing which served Christ best, and therefore good for all the members. And he expected no less from the congregation. His was what I have come to define as a parasitic church.

Thinking back over our conversation, I know that he is a good man. He was concerned that somehow he was undoing the exact purpose for which he had been called to the ministry. His problem was not organization, nor was it structure. It was perceptual. As long as the people were a means to an end, he would continue to face problems of leadership. His people were dropping out because they had burned out.

The Competitive Church

The next church on the continuum is the competitive church. It is similar in kind but less severe than the parasitic church. Several characteristics might typify such a church.

First, think in terms of the leadership of the church. The competitive church recognizes the validity of the pastor's family, but often the relationship between the two is an adversary relationship. Words such as jealousy, resentment, and bitterness typify the attitude of the pastor's family toward the church. They feel that they are competing with the church for his attention. Often he is not available for the celebration of important family events. If he has school-age children, he seldom makes an open house at the children's school.

These pastors usually feel torn between two competing loyalties. They are in a no-win position. Someone has to lose, and either way they are going to pay the price.

In terms of the competitive church's relationship to its people, they are in a race to see who can consume the resources of the family first. Whereas in the case of the parasitic church, the family is typically passive, in the competitive church the family members are resistive. They battle all the way.

In terms of space, the families agitate for less emphasis upon the place. The pastor will sometimes feel like he is in a tug-of-war. It's push and pull all the way.

In terms of time, he can seldom find a time when it is compatible to hold a meeting or initiate a program. Nothing goes down easily. The yearly church calendar comes to symbolize a pitched battle. Youth directors and leaders try to schedule more activity into a young person's life than he or she can handle, and the family is left with what is left. On the other hand, the family schedules vacations seemingly on purpose to conflict with camps and conferences.

Last of all, in terms of energy, the families guard their resources as if they were hoarding sugar. The spirit is one of possessiveness.

Faithful workers for the church are forever combing the roles, seeking new bodies to replace those who have been expended during the battle. The church's greatest problem is lack of personnel. Who will serve when the most faithful of servants have expended their all? After a few phone calls the recruiter begins to realize that the people are deciding to expend their energy elsewhere. Other commitments are given priority, and progressively the church is relegated to a lesser position. A sense of panic sets in.

From the perspective of the family, it seems that the church is constantly demanding more and more. It is as if what they have given is never enough. If it's not money, then it is time. Resentments build and a subtle sense of lethargy sets in. Motivation that once was abundant is now absent.

The Cooperative Church

Whereas the parasitic church feeds off its host and the competitive church sets up a win/lose relationship with the family, there are those churches that seek to work creatively with, rather than against, the family. I think of those churches as falling on the positive side of the continuum.

More to the center of the continuum is the cooperative church. It is the church that has a sense of relative protectiveness toward its members in terms of their family life, maybe by deciding to have no meeting one night each week. This makes sure that the family is free (as far as the church is concerned) on that night. No family member will have a committee meeting or any other meeting that night. That is certainly a beginning, but that is all it is.

Another characteristic might be the attitude of the church toward the pastoral leadership. The pastor may have a real "day off." The people may respect a sense of privacy in their leaders' lives. The church may care that the quality of life being lived by the pastors and elders is good.

When a church relates to its people as though they were children in need of parenting, it creates a sense of inequality. But in a cooperative church a more positive mind-set is fostered—where the church is the friend of the people. Between friends, people can say no without offense or tension.

Perhaps the last characteristic I would suggest for the cooperative church is the ability to be healthily other directed. By this I mean the ability of the church to define its role as being truly in the world as well as the ability to sense that the work of God is much bigger than the work of that one particular church. Cooperative churches have both a sense of near and far mission.

The concept of space as it relates to families and as it affects the church becomes a system of flexible boundaries. In the cooperative church the family would be encouraged to expand its influence in the world as a means of extending the influence of the church. The family becomes the church in the world, a legitimate means of caring outreach. The church encourages outside involvements in order to include rather than exclude the world. A cooperative church is concerned that its families flourish and sees its role as facilitating that growth and health.

In my mind a truly cooperative church does more than provide seminars on family-related topics, however basic they may be. A cooperative church defines its role in such a way that it genuinely serves its members by actively strengthening their families. If viable families are not available to some of its members, the church provides new or substitute familylike relationships and environments. The cooperative church fosters "primary" relationships between its members, not as an end in themselves but as a means to an end, the discipling of its members to Christ.

The Symbiotic Church

Farther out on the positive side of the continuum is the fourth category of church. The symbiotic church is similar to the cooperative church but differing in degree. The relationship between the church and the family is more than cooperative; it is one of mutual interdependence.

Symbiosis is an interesting word. It comes from the field of biology and refers to a dependent relationship (often beneficial) between two or more organisms.

A symbiotic relationship between the church and its families would be one in which the life of the church and the life of the family is inextricably tied to each other. If the viability of one is threatened, the life of the other is threatened as well.

It is a deadly commentary that some church leaders can trumpet distress calls on behalf of the family while at the same time proclaiming the health of the church. How can one be well if the other is sick? The answer can only be that the life of the two are not, in fact, dependent upon one another. Somehow in the minds of these leaders the one can live while the other dies or is diseased.

What I am suggesting, however, is not a change in pulpit rhetoric, but a change in philosophy in which the relationship of mutual interdependence, or symbiosis, is basic to the ministry of the church, one in which the health or disease of one is measurably experienced by the other.

Let me suggest an example.

In the New Testament the Third Letter of John is a remarkable example of the mutual interdependence of a household (that of Gaius) and the ministry of the church. Although Gaius is commended for his love and service to the church as an individual, it seems that the message embraces both Gaius and his household. Gaius and his household render "service" to the traveling evangelists who formed the cutting edge of first-century evangelism. In times of persecution the refuge of a friendly household provided welcome and needed shelter and relief.

Suppose Gaius were experiencing division and trauma within the boundaries of his household. Would he have been in a position to "render service to the brethren"? I think not. Clearly the ministry of the church was dependent upon the viability of his family. I would even go so far to say that if the first-century family as an institution had been under the kind of attack

24

threatening contemporary families, the survival of the Church would have been in question. Said another way, the Church was launched in the first century, using the hospitality of its families. Remember, there were no such things as Holiday Inns or Hilton Hotels available to those who were scattered abroad. The first buildings of the Church were the living areas of its families.

A second example comes to mind. Recently a young couple who are involved in evangelism in the Soviet Union was in our home. As a part of the evening they eagerly showed slides about their ministry. The images of one of the slides still hangs in my mind. It was a picture of a small underground church that met together in spite of incredible persecution and hostility. There they were, gathered together for a photograph standing around a small dining room table in the cramped living quarters of one of their members. On the table was a meal, a love feast, and the report of the young couple was that they had been extended remarkable hospitality in that home. They were meeting *in a home*. The vehicle of fellowship was the hospitality of that household. The "Gaius" in that house had rendered valuable service to them. The report was that although there were church buildings in the Soviet Union, they were unavailable to Evangelicals. As a result, the church was forced to meet in settings that were relatively convenient and safe. They met in homes, and they met as families. Perhaps, whenever, persecution forces the church to return to basics, we return to the natural and necessary symbiotic relationship between family and church.

Questions to Ask

Clearly I believe that the church must reevaluate its mission in light of its relationship to its families. Although the church as we know it in the Western world enjoys relative peace and freedom, part of its struggle to grow comes not from faulty methods of church growth nor from inadequate preaching, but from self-defeating philosophies of ministry that do not take into account the natural and critical importance of the family. How

25

do we evaluate our philosophy of ministry? What questions do we ask?

One answer is to use as a model the secular literature that has been generated in the area of Family Impact Analysis. This literature deals primarily with the effects of governmental policies upon the quality of family life. It is useful because it focuses upon the interface between two competing institutions—government and the family. Based upon that literature I have generated a series of questions that a church or denomination might ask itself in a manner similar to those questions asked of government. The questions are couched in the future tense although they can be asked easily in the reevaluation of existing programs. They also raise hard issues that need to be dealt with at the philosophical or policy level before any decisions in terms of programs are made.

Seven questions that require the leadership of the church to face the issues of the interface between their church and their families:

1. What is the purpose of the program, stated Biblically and in terms of your philosophy of ministry?

This question is designed to require us to think through what it is we do in light of what it is we value and believe. Latent within the question is the assumption that a church has a philosophy of ministry, one that can be stated both Biblically and pragmatically.

2. Who will be involved: As participants, both directly and indirectly? As leaders, both directly and indirectly?

The purpose of this question is to begin to ask the leaders of the church to identify the energy costs of any given program. The direct participants of any program are those who are immediately involved in the event or activity. The indirect participants are those who support the event, such as parents who car pool their children to the church for children's choir, or custodians who clean up after a church social.

It is not difficult to measure the direct involvement of members of any particular event, but it is perhaps even more crucial

26

to measure the indirect participation. My hunch is that when people in the church burn out they do so because of inordinate, indirect energy costs, often for which there are only indirect benefits or gains. It is difficult to stay motivated when there is a great deal of energy loss without the rewards that come from direct involvement.

In terms of the leadership, it is again much easier to measure the energy costs of those who are directly involved such as the deacons who call on visitors on a weekday evening, but it is more difficult to measure the energy costs of those who participate at the policy or governance level, such as official boards.

3. What will be the "money" costs of the program, the participants, and the church?

In terms of the pragmatics of ministry, money is often the bottom line. Unfortunately, churches frequently do not have an accurate picture of what it really costs to run a program.

Let me give an example.

Early in my ministry I served on the staff of a large church as an associate pastor. My job description included supervising a family counseling center and directing the young adult ministries. In discussing the philosophy of the counseling center, one of the pastors of the church resisted the idea of charging fees. He believed that the church should offer counseling "free." I can still remember the look on his face when I reminded him that he did not work for free and that someone was paying for the services he provided. The service still cost money and somebody paid. He later confided to me that he had always thought of those services as being free even though they obviously did cost money. There is, in fact, no such thing as a free lunch. Somebody pays and the church needs to ask itself if those costs should be borne directly by the participants or indirectly by the body as a whole.

There is another dimension that needs to be considered in the financial costs of an event or program. It has to do with the cumulative expenses that develop over time.

For example, a family with four children ages 12 through 18 might earnestly desire that their children participate actively in the youth programs of their church. On the other hand, a zealous youth director might schedule several expensive or even inexpensive events every month—events whose cumulative expense can run into much more money than the family has to spend on recreation. The parents face the dilemma of saying no or saying "you pay" and thus run the risk of creating a disincentive for the kids. If the church intends to put families into that position, it ought to be a deliberate rather than a casual decision. Families just don't have the discretionary money they once had. Inflation has seen to that.

4. *What will be the time costs in terms of daily schedules, weekly schedules, and the yearly calendar?*

The purpose of this question is to force a review of the time demands made upon the family. Just because the pace of life in the Western world is increasing at breakneck speed doesn't mean that the church must contribute to the problem.

This is the place where the church easily becomes competitive. I know of a church that deliberately spreads its summer camps for its youth throughout the summer so as to be able to have something going on all summer long. The problem is that they effectively prevent families with several children from taking vacations together. Families either take their vacation while someone is at camp or someone has to miss going to camp. The families should never have been forced to make that choice.

5. *How will it affect other programs in the family, in the church, and in the community?*

This question is designed to provoke thought and discussion on the integration of the Christian life and the secular world. It has as its backdrop the teaching of Christ that we are to be salt and light. Also that we dwell together in unity.

How many meetings have been canceled at the last moment because someone discovered a schedule conflict with another program in the church? But what about conflicts with other programs in the community? The purpose of the question is to see that the issue is raised, not how it is answered.

6. *What are the alternatives to the program or the event?*

Unnecessary duplication of a program offered by someone else is unconscionable. Inefficiency is not the best use of the Lord's money. But, let's face it. It's very threatening to cooper-

28

ate with others and risk the exposure of our people to other leaders and settings.

7. What will be the benefits of the program to the participants, to the family, and to the church?

It is never wrong to lobby strongly for what you want. This question is designed to provide the opportunity to set forth the best case.

The Family Impact Analysis is designed to prepare a church to make wise decisions about activities relevant to the quality of life for its families. It is not intended to stop anything that is consistent with God's purposes in the world, but rather to help churches say yes to the right things.

In addition to the Family Impact Analysis I would suggest three other important issues that should be considered.

I think every church should have a family ombudsman. An ombudsman is an advocate, someone who represents the positions of a particular group or interest. In this case, the church would tacitly admit to itself that its institutional momentum can lead to decisions that are not in the best interest of the family. In one sense we need to be protected from ourselves. Although the family is a "consumer" of church "goods," the family's best interests are not automatically being served. Someone needs to be assigned the task of advocacy and have access to the decision-making processes of the church.

My second thought has to do with the assumptions that undergird family ministry. Few of us would disagree that something more needs to be done. But what?

One answer is to rethink the assumptions that predetermine adult education in the church. Adult education like most of the education ministry of the church has been patterned after the educational establishment in the secular world. It is no secret that the secular educational establishment has concluded, at least tentatively, that the family as we know it has become outmoded. Therefore, skills for competent family living are not emphasized. Adults are not led to understand the difference between education and socialization. (This difference will be discussed at length in the next chapter.)

If the task of the church is the *socialization* of its members into the Kingdom of God; then the chief agent for socialization (the family) will be seen as crucial.

If, on the other hand, the task of the church is seen to be *education,* then the chief agent for that process (classes, programs, teachings, activities) will be emphasized. Our assumptions determine the direction of our ministry.

The third issue has to do with the emergence of a new area of specialization in the ministry of the church, that of marriage and family.

Although some large churches are beginning to see the need for this emphasis, the jobs are often filled by those who are not trained for the task. Their motivations are high, and their dedication unquestioned. But the task is too critical to be assigned to someone who has not garnered the skills needed to do an effective job. Bluntly said, without retraining, we cannot afford to give the task to youth pastors who are no longer young or returned missionaries who cannot for some reason continue on in the mission field.

My analysis leads me to define the task of marriage and family ministry as a two-dimensioned specialization. The two dimensions are the preventive and the corrective.

The preventive dimension of marriage and family ministry requires the understanding of and the skills to stimulate the socialization tasks of the family. It is the adult education function of the church with a new wrinkle. The person who is adept in the preventive task of marriage and family ministry understands both why and how families work as they do. These specialists understand the function and role of the family in the broader society. And they understand the task of the Church and its interdependence with the family. The preventive encompasses more than offering family-related courses during the Sunday school hour. It involves the ability to articulate the mission of the church and the mission of the family in compatible terms and the ability to structure a ministry designed to facilitate those missions.

The second dimension in a marriage and family ministry is the corrective. Although the church has seen the need for pastoral counseling for years, the corrective task in my opinion is markedly different from the traditional models used in pastoral counseling. The corrective task of marriage and family ministry should be relational and interactional. The skills needed to fulfill this task, therefore, emerge from the combined disciplines of sociology and psychology. The corrective task demands the ability to both understand and mediate the family as a system. (The concept of system will be discussed in Chapter 6.)

It also involves the ability to facilitate short-term or brief therapies and to deal effectively with most crises that are experienced by the family.

Thus the new breed of marriage and family ministers should be able to handle 80 percent of the counseling problems that walk in the front door of the church and to know when and where to refer the others. They ought not to be rookies. Their training should involve their direct and rigorous participation in the counseling task and extensive supervision of that counseling. They should have already confronted the system dynamics of their own families of origin. They should feel comfortable with themselves as persons and feel at ease in their counseling role.

What I am suggesting is that we cannot afford to foster the neglect of the family by giving it anything other than our best in terms of the kind of people who enter that ministry. The demands of the twentieth century upon the family require that we commit ourselves fully to the task and open ourselves to redefining and restructuring the traditional roles in the church.

We must call for the best and we must give them room to do their work for God.

4

Our Task, Their Needs

What does a ministry to the family look like? What are the specifics? What sets such a ministry apart from other approaches to ministry?

As I suggested before, for a ministry to families to build strength in the family (that is to be preventive), attention must be paid to the socialization task of the family. Socialization, however, is not a static term. It is a dynamic process. By dynamic I mean that socialization tasks change over time. The tasks in the early years of the marriage are not the same as the tasks in the retirement years. As a result we must understand not only the concept of socialization, we must also understand how families change over time. This latter function is best described in the literature having to do with the life cycle of the family.

Recent years have brought forth a plethora of books about the life cycle of the family, both from the popular and the technical points of view. But little has been done to integrate this information into the warp and woof of the churches' ministry. In this chapter I hope to establish the interface between the task of socialization and the life cycle of the family and to suggest how the combined product of the two provides us with a working model for marriage and family ministries in the church.

Understanding the Task of Socialization

Socialization was defined in Chapter 2 as "the process by which persons acquire the knowledge, skills, and dispositions that make them more or less able members of their society." The question that immediately arises is, how does the person do this?

To begin with a person needs to acquire the language system inherent to his or her society. Language is the vehicle of culture and enables the person to perform at least two necessary functions within that culture.

First, language has a sorting function which allows the person to discriminate between objects in the world. Language as words thus allows the person to prioritize the objects in his or her world according to the value system of the culture. We learn to value one color over another; to like the taste of certain foods over others, etc. The ability to assign meaning to objects provides the person with the ability to organize the personal, social, as well as the physical geography of his or her world.

Objects are not only material in the sense of tables and chairs. They are also immaterial in the sense of truth and justice. Language as words provides the opportunity to see, to hear, and to feel what is immaterial but "really" out there in the world.

I remember, for example, the first time I understood the concept of grace. I was a young high school senior, impressed with my ability to sort through the particulars in my world. I was not a Christian. My understanding of religion was predicated upon the concept of works, although I didn't have a word to describe it. I thought that if I were fair to my fellowman and if at the end of my life the good outweighed the bad, I was home free. God was obligated to accept me.

Then I came face-to-face with that terrible verse in the book of Romans: "The wages of sin is death; but the gift of God is eternal life through Jesus Christ our Lord." I hated the word death. Several months before, three members of my family had died within a six-week time span. An uncle, a cousin, and my grandfather had all died suddenly. Psychologically I was still reeling. Then to hear that I, too, would die because of my sin was more than I could bear. My first reaction was to protest, to rationalize. But the reality of my sin was there. I couldn't deny it.

I can still remember the soaring feeling that lifted me up one Sunday morning as I heard a sermon on the word *grace*. I'm sure that I had heard the word before, and I'm sure that I had used the word, but never in the sense that it was being used that Sunday morning. Grace was God's dealing with me not as I deserved but lovingly because of Jesus Christ. Grace was God's giving me something I could never earn, new life in Christ. There it was. An immaterial object (grace) that had always existed but not as a part of my world. My becoming a Christian involved the acquisition of new words and their meanings. I had to learn a new language system in order to sort out the world as God sorts it out. Such is the process of illumination, the Holy Spirit's bringing the unbeliever to a place where Jesus Christ, the Light of the World, is perceived through the enlightenment of the Word of God.

The second function that language provides is an organizing function. Language has a grammar. Language provides rules that define the ability to think and to create order between the objects in the person's world. Language gives us the capacity of perspective, the ability to see objects in relationship to one another. It is the grammar of one's language system that allows for the creative response to the environment. Whereas language as words gives us the ability to perceive the building blocks of our world, language as grammar gives us the ability to organize those building blocks into meaningful patterns.

Perhaps it is in an understanding of the function of language and the task of socialization that the controversy surrounding the nature of conversion can be sorted out. A recent *Christianity Today* editorial identified the tension between a conversionist definition of salvation and an orthodox definition. The conversionist pointed to the event, usually experienced by a young adult, while the orthodox pointed to the process, usually begun as a child. The editorial held both expressions of what it meant to be born again to be valid, but the conversionist position seemed to deny the validity of the orthodox definition, and the orthodox held the conversionist to be true only in part.

The dilemma is bridged if one comes to see that a child raised in a Christian home can have the use of the language of salvation as well as the appropriate faith response to that language from a very early age. Thus it is true that some Christians cannot remember when they weren't Christians, especially if they were exposed to the truth of the Gospel and the words and grammar of Christianity as a natural part of their acquisition of language as a whole. They can no more remember when they became Christians than they can remember when they began to talk.

On the other hand, there are those who even though they have been brought up in a religious home failed to grasp the meaning of the words or at least refused to respond to those meanings. Still others can be raised without the use of the words or the grammar and be completely secular. Salvation for these two groups would of necessity require a conversionist response.

34

Either way salvation involves a process, sometimes culminated by an event, in which the person by faith responds to the Word of God. Evangelism—whether of children, youth, or adults—is a socialization task involving the transmittal of language skills to the person so that he or she by faith responds appropriately to the Word of God. The follow-up of new believers becomes the steady providing of skills and abilities to understand the Word of God. It is the learning of a new language, both the words and the grammar. It is the introduction into a new culture, one that is very broad in some ways and very narrow in others.

I only remind the reader of what has already been said in Chapter 2. Where are the natural skills of language normally acquired? They are essentially acquired in the context of the primary relationship of the family. Therefore, it makes good sense for the church to strengthen that natural ally. Our task becomes one of making families stronger rather than attempting to do the job without them.

Implications for Christian Education

However, the implications of the above discussion are broader than their impact upon marriage and family ministries. The discussion has broad Christian education implications as well.

We are all concerned with the rate of attrition of those who as adults or young adults seem to fall away from the faith. What can be done to help them "stick"; that is, to continue on in their journey as Christians?

A partial answer lies in the socialization of the new believers into the Christian society. They must be helped to use and understand a new language system. Unfortunately, many are left to learn the language on their own. I don't need to dwell on how difficult that task is. Anyone who has stumbled around in a foreign country without the ability to speak the language can empathize. When you are on your own without an interpreter you feel lost. So it is with new believers. They are lost without an interpreter. In that sense the discipler is like an interpreter and a teacher of the new language.

A second implication has to do with the relative level of difficulty of education materials. I frankly don't think that the Christian education establishment has yet come to grips with the problem of the relative levels of Christian maturity of adults and young adults. Even though a person has the ability to speak and think in English, that doesn't mean the person has the ability to speak and think in the language of Christianity. Also, when you begin to use any new language you need to begin with "Dick and Jane" kinds of reading material. Although most of us can read, many of us are illiterate when it comes to an appropriate use of the language of Christianity. Much, much work and research still need to be done regarding this issue.

The third, and last, implication has to do with the context within which the new language is learned. It is next to impossible to learn a new language only using objective materials. If all you have are written materials you'll never learn to speak. Even if you have audio tapes you will struggle. The best solution is to live in the country where the language is spoken, and it is even better to live with a family who speaks the language. There is something about primary relationships that makes the task of learning a new language easier.

So it is with learning the language of Christianity. When you are accepted as one of the family and are encompassed by the family as you learn the new language, you will more likely persist in your commitment to that new society. You are more likely to "stick." Said in another way, information without relationship is ultimately useless.

The acquisition of a new language is only the first step in the task of socialization. The additional dimensions of socialization have been identified in the secular literature. One author in particular has set forth the issues in an especially helpful way. Orville Brim writing in the book *Socialization After Childhood* says,

> There are three things a person requires before he is able to perform satisfactorily in a role. He must know what is expected of him (both in behavior and values), must be able to meet the role requirements, and must desire to practice the behavior and pursue

appropriate ends. It can be said that the purposes of
socialization are to give a person knowledge, ability
and motivation (p. 25).

If we stop with knowledge or information, we have only
completed a third of the task. Socialization demands that a
person have the ability to act on the information and the motivation to do so. What good is it if you know that you need to
change but lack the skills to do something differently? It does
you no good at all.

Brim has provided a useful model for the socialization task.

Figure One	Behavior	Values
Knowledge	A	B
Ability	C	D
Motivation	E	F

In this model knowledge is the content or the information
needed to accomplish a particular task. Ability is the skill to be
able to do it. And motivation is the "want to" to do it.

The behavior column is equivalent to the "what" and the
values column is the "why."

Thus, a new recruit in the Army must know what he must do
(A) and why that is important (B). He must know how to do
what he must do (C) and why that is important (D). And last of
all he must want to do what he is to do (E) and why that is
important (F).

Brim's model is extremely powerful and useful in the analysis
of every task that an adult must learn. Let's look at a few and
practice using the model.

A young couple comes to you and wants to get married. You
are their pastor and want the very best for them. Where do you

begin? Probably you begin at the knowledge level, A and B. You give them information about what it means to be married such as becoming a new entity, getting along with in-laws, financial management, conflict resolution, and making love. You also try to convince them that it is important for them to read what you have given them. But you know that you need to go beyond knowledge to the skills level.

You also assume that they are motivated to read the material, but often you find that you are wrong. Most young couples overestimate both their knowledge and their abilities. As a result they are undermotivated.

This is why I have moved to "postmarital" counseling. Let me explain.

When a couple approaches me to marry them, I require one or two sessions before they marry. The purpose of these times is to do a kind of preliminary screening of the couple. Are they Christians? Is one or the other emotionally unstable or blatantly unprepared for marriage? What are their plans for the ceremony? I then schedule them for a 5,000-mile checkup and a 10,000-mile checkup, sessions to come after they are married at the three-month anniversary and at the sixth-month. I use the analogy of the preventive maintenance they practice on a new car. The postmarital sessions are intentionally preventive.

My experience has been that when they return for their 5,000-mile checkup and especially for their 10,000-mile one, they are highly motivated both to learn what they don't know and their lack of skills has surfaced as well. Now I know they are at a place where they can practice their skills in a meaningful context.

Two benefits seem to surface. First, we can dwell on the areas where they are hurting and forget those areas where they seem to be doing well. That's more efficient. Secondly, we are able to deal with problem areas before they become too severe in nature. The 5,000-mile and 10,000-mile checkups act like an early warning system and head off problems before they get too sticky and involved.

Two other examples are useful to point out the differences between the various components of Brim's model.

Suppose you are an adult education director and you decide to develop a life-related study for two separate age groups in your church. The first group is new parents with their first child. The task you are concerned with for them is toilet training. The second group is adults in the preretirement years. Your concern for them is the preparation of a will. An analysis of the socialization tasks using Brim's model asks, is the problem a lack of knowledge, a lack of skills, or a lack of motivation? Probably in the case of the new parents, they are very motivated to toilet train their children. They are sick and tired of diapers. So motivation is not their problem. They just lack the "how-to." So the unit would best pay attention to building skills with practical demonstrations from experienced parents.

On the other hand, the mature adult without a will suffers not only from a lack of knowledge but also from a lack of motivation. To make a will is to acknowledge one's own mortality. It is to face the likelihood of one's own death. Thus the special problem for each task can be thought through and appropriate steps taken in terms of the lesson.

In order for a ministry to families in the church to be effective, it must respond creatively to the particular demands of each situation. Our hackneyed approach of throwing information at every issue may be useless. What is needed is an intelligent analysis of the special demands made by each situation.

Families Change;
So Must the Church

5

Families change over time. Their experience is like the tides that ebb and flow at the seashore. There are predictable times and predictable levels. But every wave is different, and every tide leaves a unique mark upon the sand. Life, like the sea, is infinitely variable yet uncannily routine and ordinary.

A ministry to families must be able to take advantage of the predictability of the life cycle, yet do so in an interesting manner. Real life need not be boring. There is infinite drama. However, it is strangely comforting when we learn that others have experienced or are experiencing the same growing pains that we are, that someone else has been through the waters before us and survived.

I am reminded of a family trip down the rapids of the Colorado River. Our white water experience was the trip of a lifetime. Others had gone before, but when we faced the river on our first day, we were all revved up, motors running, ready to take the river on.

When we entered the second rapid, we experienced our baptism of fire. Our two daughters, ages 11 and 16, were washed overboard. They were riding with me on the outside pontoons of the raft, and a wave came from the other side and hosed them off. My oldest daughter grabbed her sister with one hand and the raft with the other as we tried to pull them back inside the boat. The raft pitched wildly. Shannon, our youngest, screamed hysterically, but Sheryl held on with all her might. My wife, Lucy, and I pulled and tugged at the two bobbing heads in the water. Finally, we prevailed, and the two girls were returned to safety, inside the raft.

Their bodies were cold from the 55-degree water and their psyches were traumatized. The rest of the day they rode the rapids from the relative safety of the inside of the boat. We had all learned a lesson: never underestimate the river.

The next day we were prepared. We had survived our accident, and we were stronger for it. The experience was recorded in our memory banks, and we were ready to move on. The second day brought us to Crystal Rapid. It's white water rating was an eight or a nine (out of a maximum rating of ten), depending on the time of the year.

As our boatman circled in the quiet water just before the rapid, he explained his strategy for navigating it. About a third of the way through, he would spin the raft full circle in order to miss a very bad hole, one that spilled inexperienced travelers.

We entered the rapid and the raft began to rise and pitch like a bucking horse. Suddenly, as he predicted, he swung the boat 360 degrees and we all yelped with excitement. We missed the deadly hole and finished our ride without incident. His prior experience, as well as others who had gone through before, provided us with a seasoned guide and a strategy for handling the danger. Because of his expertise, we survived Crystal. Had we tried it on our own, we would have been swamped.

Life in families is like that river. There are predictable rapids each with a measurable level of difficulty. The odd fact is that while we take advantage of the expertise of experienced boatmen in many spheres of our lives, when it comes to transversing the predictable crises in the life cycle of the family, each family is expected to find its own way through. Unfortunately, and unnecessarily, many are swamped.

The blunt fact is that no institution in society is preparing the family to navigate the waters of its life cycle. Each stage of the life cycle demands new roles, and the neophyte is expected to survive on his or her own. Only, perhaps, in the case of premarital counseling is the church involved in anticipating the dangers that lie ahead and providing needed information about the future.

But what about the other stages? Who teaches young parents how to survive the intrusion of a squalling infant into the relative tranquillity of their lives? Who prepares parents to handle the storms of adolescence or the uncertainty of mid-life? Such help is too rare.

It is this vacuum that provides the church with its most exciting opportunity for ministry today. The knowledge, skills, and motivation to cope with the predictable crises of the life cycle are the cups of cold water to be given in Jesus' name for this generation.

Researchers in the fields of family sociology and family

psychology have been busy for decades studying and collating data about these "rapids." The information is there. Our problem is not what to do; it is, who will do it?

This chapter is designed to stimulate thought in terms of the stages of the life cycle and the predictable role changes associated with each. We must adapt our methods to fit the realities of people's lives as they live in families. People have much in common with those who are in the same stage of the life cycle, irrespective of how old they are or even what social class they are. Common experiences in families are a great leveler.

It is a fact. When adults, whether young or old, married or single, sit and talk to one another about families, their focus is upon stages, not ages.

However, in contrast, most materials in the field of family education are written from a topical point of view. Take the issue of communication. It is usually dealt with across the life cycle even though the communication demands of a couple are different at one stage than another. Or take the books on sex. Most are written as if sex in marriage does not change according to how old you are or how long you've been married. However, sex in marriage does change, just like people change, and those changes are important to know. But if we teach without reference to these differences, we are less than effective.

The literature that is important in understanding how families change over time is the literature on the life cycle of the family. For purposes of the model I intend to develop for this chapter, the work of Evelyn Duvall is most central. Duvall was clearly the first and most influential author to elaborate the concept of the life cycle of the family. According to this theory, a new stage of the life cycle is reached when a person or married couple is required to function in a new role, using information and skills that were not used or needed previously. Thus, each new stage of the life cycle demands new information and/or skills from the stage before. Each new stage is demarcated from the previous stage based upon the introduction of a new role, and each role requires different or additional skills. What is needed is a strategy for preventive family life education in the church that provokes families to anticipate the demands of the approaching stage in the life cycle as well as provides support during their present stage.

A Model for Marriage and Family Ministry

Table I summarizes a useful model for looking at the family and the church. It is designed to integrate the issues of socialization with the life cycle. The questions at the bottom are meant to provoke the kind of interaction which promotes healthy discussion and facilitates healthy change. They are meant to provoke interaction in terms of felt needs.

Table I

MARRIAGE AND FAMILY MINISTRY IN THE LOCAL CHURCH

A. The Beginning Years
  1. Between Families
  2. Neo-Marital
  3. Neo-Parental

B. The Building Years
  4. Young Children
  5. First Teenager

C. The Maturing Years
  6. Empty Nest
  7. Retirement

D. The Single Years
  8. Single Person
  9. Single Parent

- What does the person need to know in order to function effectively in the present stage?
- What are the skills needed in order to do a good job?
- Does the person really want to deal with the issues relevant to this stage?
- How is it going? What is normal? What is abnormal? If needed, who can help?
- What comes next? How can one plan for the future?

This model suggests that the socialization processes that are critical in the effective development of the family over time cluster themselves into four natural categories or groups of related tasks with subcategories reflected in the stage of the life cycle. I have chosen to think of them as the Beginning Years, the Building Years, the Maturing Years, and the Single Years. The categories are not absolute but heuristic, that is, labeled so as to be easy to remember. Let me briefly describe each larger grouping from the standpoint of the primary task or tasks that are especially important to each, with an even briefer word about the pragmatics of ministry peculiar to each.

A. The Beginning Years

"In the beginning God created . . . ." There's something exciting about beginnings, whether it is the beginning of the earth and the people that live on it or the beginning of life together as a married couple. There is something pristine about the newness of beginnings. The young are usually optimistic and fresh with the promise of life. They are tender and inexperienced yet usually unaware of their naiveté.

The beginning years are like freshly turned soil ready for planting. Much work is ahead, but the young are poised for sowing and the promise of harvest in the future. Those of us who have lived through other harvests with their disappointments and failures must avoid blunting the enthusiasm of those who are beginning. Although we are veterans, our experience must not diminish their enthusiasm for the tasks that lie before them. That enthusiasm, when tempered with experience, will become the wisdom for the generations that are to follow.

Our task is to do more than was done for us. Or if it was done well, to repeat the experience and improve on it, if possible.

Family ministry for this cluster of stages starts with the task of encouraging the young single adult to become a whole and distinct person and ends with the young couple and their first child. People must learn to be independent before they can learn to be interdependent. They must learn to make a wise choice of a mate and be open to that mate.

44

The Beginning Years are full of hope and fervency. They are also years full of turmoil and tension for some. Generally they are years of ambivalence, of seemingly mutually exclusive emotions such as love and hate, trust and fear.

Leading young adults through the Beginning Years is a task similar to that of coaching. You can provide them with the necessary plays but you cannot play the game for them. The ball is in their hands, and they must learn to take responsibility for the outcome. The frustration for the coach is to watch from the sidelines and then be able to handle the thrill of victory as well as the agony of defeat.

Recent literature in the social and behavioral sciences has identified the single most important task for the young person during the Beginning Years as the task of differentiating oneself from one's family of origin. One theory in psychology holds that it is necessary for a young person in this stage to experience some kind of rebellion in order to become a healthy and mature adult. There is another, emerging opinion that disputes this kind of determinism. It is the literature of family systems theory as defined by the work of Murray Bowen. This position holds that a family naturally has a kind of emotional stickiness to it. The relationship between the parents and the young adult in the Beginning Years is often defined by the parents' ability or inability to release the young adult to become his or her own person and to become a person who is independent and responsible.

Anyone who has worked with families long enough knows that this is not an easy task. If you are the parents, how do you let go? If you are the young adult, how do you get them to let you go?

The answer to these questions begins with the need for the young adult to accept responsibility for his or her relationships with parents and siblings. As children it is natural either to assume that someone else will take care of the well-being of relationships or to assume passively that nothing can be done. Both assumptions are wrong for an adult. Part of becoming a responsible adult is the decision to take charge of one's own life and the relationships with the people in it. That decision involves one's relationship with God as well. Many young people, in order to demonstrate their supposed independence from their families, rebel against God as a means of rebelling against their families. They make the mistake of throwing the baby out with the bathwater. Differentiating oneself involves treating all relationships as if they are separate and distinct.

According to family systems theory, the usual alternatives to differentiation are to err in one of two extremes: to become disengaged or to stay enmeshed.

To become disengaged is to become an unplugged kind of person, one who handles the problems of relationships by walking away from them. It is the position of the prodigal son in Luke 15. He thought that he could solve whatever problems he had at home by running away from them and from the relationship with his father. But when he got to the far country he found that his problems had increased and that his father was psychologically still with him. In the midst of his struggles, he had a conversation with his father in his head. What an irony. He had run away, putting miles of distance between himself and his father, only to find that his father was right there with him. To unplug and disengage rarely solves any problem. It usually makes things worse.

At the other extreme is the response of enmeshment. Enmeshed people are so stuck to their families of origin that they never become truly separate and distinct people. The emotional stickiness in the family holds people bound to the family so that they find it painful to be independent. It is the story of the elder son in Luke 15, who has never left home.

The enmeshed person might be characterized by compulsive patterns of communication such as needing to talk with a parent every day by phone or needing to visit the parent every week.

It is my opinion that in order for a person to have the freedom at the time of marriage to "leave Father and Mother and to cleave to his wife," the process of differentiation must have been effectively begun. Thus, the stakes are high.

To be a separate, distinct, differentiated person is the Biblical norm. To be disengaged or to remain enmeshed is not. The task of differentiation is the major task of the Beginning Years.

46

I have suggested that the primary task of the Beginning Years is the differentiation of the people from their family of origin. The importance of the task can be seen in the three stages of the life cycle that make up the Beginning Years.

1. Between Families

The Between Families young adult is faced with the task of becoming a responsible and independent person. It is frightening that in our Western culture we have placed such responsibility on the shoulders of that young person. Decisions having to do with whether to marry, choice of mate, choice of career, whether or not to have children, when to have children, where to live, are all critical in their import for the future.

The Between Families young adult faced with making the above decisions must be mentored so as to make the best decisions that he or she can make. That is the opportunity for the Church in its ministry to the young person in this stage of life. The need lies in the significance of the decisions that will soon be made. The opportunity for ministry lies in the development of relationships between the young adult and significant others whose experience and quality of life will be seen by the young adult to be copyable. It is a time for Pauls and Timothys. It is a time for words of challenge such as, "Follow me even as I follow Christ."

2. Neo-Marital

The Beginning Years young adult who chooses to marry is faced with another significant task, that of learning the new role of husband or wife. The difficulty of the task lies in the Biblical model in the Book of Genesis, "for this cause a man shall leave his father and mother and shall cleave to his wife." "Leave" can be thought of as the task of differentiation. Many marriages fail because the husband or the wife or both have never come to the place where they have "left" their families of origin so as to be free to form a new family. The bonding of "becoming one

47

flesh," i.e., "cleaving," is hindered or inhibited by the failure to have worked through the issue of differentiation. Thus, the young marriages that suffer from irresponsibility, hyper-independence, failures in intimacy, etc., at the one extreme, and possessiveness, dependency, and the need to dominate and control at the other extreme, are infected with a marriage-threatening disease from the onset.

The opportunity for ministry by the Church to the Neo-Marital young adult includes modeling of married relationships that have somehow dealt with the issues of leaving and cleaving. The miracle of "becoming one flesh" and the mystery that infuses marriage needs to be demonstrated in the lives of veteran couples who have weathered the storms of the first years and have gained by their experience. Newly married young adults don't need to be constantly hit over the head with what they should do. They can probably quote the ideals to us verbatim. What they need most of all is hope. Is it possible in this day and age to create a marriage that works? One that meets the needs of its participants and possesses the ability to flex with the ebb and flow of the future? Said in another way, they don't need to be led by perfect people with perfect marriages. They need to be led by real people who are survivors, whose marriages, by the grace of God, are getting better, people who love each other and see marriage as a process of becoming.

3. Neo-Parental

The third stage in the Beginning Years is the couple with their first child. What do they need? They, too, need hope and affirming direction. The despair of the newly married young adult is the dismal statistics of divorce. The despair of the new parent is the horror stories of teenager rebellion and parental failures. Is it possible to bring a child up in today's world and have that child love and honor his or her parents? What is the "discipline and instruction of the Lord" in which children are to be raised? How does one keep the marriage fresh and alive when everything around makes such intense demands, especially the new baby and the new career?

48

The opportunity for the Church in this stage is not only to provide effective role models for parenting but also to provide new kinship structures within the Church to take up the slack many new parents feel in the inadequacy of their natural, extended family. Young married couples provide the best opportunity for the Church to become the new community or family of God for the couple. Because so many of them are isolated or alienated from their families of origin, they really do need one another. With just a little bit of encouragement they will care for one another's children, they will help one another move, they will creatively respond to one another in whatever needs they seem to have. They will be the Church to one another.

And, where the natural families of origin are within the same church, guidance can be given to capitalize on those natural relationships in a healthy and helpful manner.

Last of all the Church can help the young couple look to the future with hope. Rather than anticipating that their children will bring agony in years to come, as is the case with many young couples, we can offer them the assurance that the Church as the new family of God will be there with them as they transit the coming rapids with their children. They will not be alone.

B. The Building Years

When my two daughters entered adolescence, I had similar talks with each of them. The situation involved their feeling overwhelmed by the thought of leaving the relative comfort and security of their childhood years. At appropriate times I sat with each of them and talked about the bridge they were about to cross. On the one side of the bridge was their childhood. It had been a time of fun, games, laughter, and, for the most part, happiness. Of course there had been trauma, but on the whole theirs had been a happy childhood. Now they were faced with the prospect of growing and changing bodies, junior high school, boys, dating, demanding relationships, and the insecurity of transversing new territory yet unexplored by them. Each in her own way was immobilized by the thought of the future.

Beyond the end of the bridge called adolescence was the prospect of adulthood. Neither child was all that enamored with the thought of growing up. The adult world must have seemed very threatening indeed. Wars, assassinations, crime, brutality, violence, all were a daily part of their world either through the stories they heard or the media that touched their lives. I could empathize with their fears. They had reason to be afraid. The world was, in fact, crazy and seemed upside down at times.

However, they couldn't avoid crossing that bridge. If they were to pass successfully through the rapids of adolescence, and if we were to ride the waves with them, we all needed to understand the nature of the bridge they were crossing and the implications both for them and for us. The norm would be ambivalence rather than comfort. There was risk for both of us rather than security. It would be the best of times and the worst of times . . . all at the same time. Who wouldn't be afraid?

As I listened to them, I tried to understand their ambivalence and to encourage them to launch out onto their trek with vigor, an attitude they had seen modeled by their mother. Their bridge was for crossing, and the crossing would be a time of exhilarating challenge.

A strange phenomenon occurred following my conversations with my second daughter. I was contacted by my high school graduating class to bring a few words of inspiration for our 25th-year class reunion. I had agreed and then set about deciding what I would say. My mind ranged far and wide for an appropriate story. I kept coming back to the conversations with my daughters.

It occurred to me that in the Building Years of our lives, we were on another bridge, not the bridge between childhood and adulthood, but the bridge between youth and aging. But who would sit down with us and talk about the ambivalence we faced? Probably no one. Unfortunately, many of us would stumble through divorces, remarriages, mid-life crises, and other various anxiety states without anyone to guide us.

I think that the Building Years, the stages of the family with young children and then their first adolescent, are years that require the crossing of two bridges simultaneously. We must prepare our children to cross their bridge called adolescence while at the same time we prepare ourselves to cross the bridge from youth to begin our aging years. It is normal to experience a double portion of ambivalence. It is also a time of great joy and, for many, a time of great heartache. By definition, however, it cannot be a time of total tranquillity, not if we are dealing with our own feelings honestly and allowing others to deal with theirs openly as well. We need not be defeated by the prospect of our bridge. It is as illogical for me to deny my own aging as it would be for me to try to keep my child a child beyond the time it is appropriate for him or her to grow up.

Perhaps that's what the Building Years are all about. It is not a time of growing up but a time of growing on. It is a time of making peace with oneself about the realities of life. Your children are growing up and you need to let them grow and go. The temptation is to prevent growing on by using one or both of two ploys. The first is to try to stay young yourself by denying the realities of age. One may so identify with the youth culture that one prolongs adolescent behavior and irresponsibility to the realities of the adult life. The second is to keep your own children from becoming adolescents by perpetuating their childishness. As long as they stay children, they can't have mothers or fathers who have aged. Either ploy achieves the same end: the inappropriate holding on to youth rather than the natural releasing of the young and a graceful embrace of the future.

4. Young Children

To the families in the Young Children stage, it may seem incongruous to be thinking of growing old. The reality is that now is the time to begin. Families with young children can become so overwhelmed with the details of daily life and the demands of keeping it all together that they lose perspective on the nature of time. So often parents with kids who have grown up and left the home say, "Where did the time go? Why didn't we change when we had the chance?"

I remember walking into our children's bedroom when they

51

were very young. Lucy, my wife, was standing at the window watching them play in the outside yard. As I stood at her side I realized she was weeping. "Why are you crying?" "I'm just telling myself that I have to let them grow up and go away. I'm getting myself ready."

They were mere babies, yet she was instinctively preparing herself to release them from her parental bonds to the freedom of being responsible adults. "Too soon," you say. I would disagree. More of us begin the process too late than too early.

5. First Teenager Stage

To the families with their first teenager, it is more natural to speak of growing old. Often your first clue to your own aging is the growing awareness that your parents who have always been the paragons of vigor and health are beginning to experience the limitations of their own age. Health problems, looming retirement, and the death of friends and relatives who were once so young filters into their daily conversation. Their awareness of the process contributes to your own awareness.

How you handle the bridge of the Building Years affects not only how you relate to your own children as they transit adolescence, it also affects how you relate to your aging parents. I'm convinced that part of the problem with the isolation of the aging members of our society and the neglect of some of them by their children is the preoccupation of those in the Building Years with staying young themselves. How can you stay young if your parents are old? You can't. The response then is to deny your own age by denying their existence. If you stay in relationship with them, you must face what is really happening. You cannot avoid it. They are aging, and so are you.

What I am suggesting is paradoxical. If, in the Building Years, you concentrate only on what is directly before you, you will likely achieve exactly the opposite of what you want. If, on the other hand, you accept and flow with the swell of the years, you will be a more comfortable person in your own right and certainly be much more comfortable to live with. Those who live with you will receive the benefits of that comfort.

It is a time for crossing two bridges and a time of exhilaration.

The Church's ministry to families in the Young Children stage through the First Teenager stage is similar. It has to do with providing meaningful networks of support so that the normal storms of these years can be weathered appropriately and with dignity.

How do you know what is normal? What are the practical strategies that help us cope with our emerging children? Where can you go for help? When do you need to go? How do you cope with the normal dislocations of these times? It is a time of transition for everybody, and as such, it is a time of tension.

The natural tendency in a society where feelings and fears are not shared freely is to close yourself off from others, to try to cope on your own. The magnificence of a caring community of people who are with you in the midst of your struggles is that you are not alone and therefore much of the stress can be shared and ventilated. Again, it is the Church in action in the twentieth century. It is the Body of Christ alive today ministering where people are hurting. It is the ministry of the Holy Spirit fleshed out in the lives of fellow travelers who want the best for you and are able to accept you as you are even when you are not what you ought to be.

Like life on any bridge, it is a time of ambivalence. The person must face two ways simultaneously. The adult in the Building Years must face toward adolescent children and toward aging parents. It is a time of high demand and a time when it is very difficult to forgive oneself. It is more natural to be either defensive or to be self-critical. It is a time for the incarnation of Christ to take on new significance through the care given by friends.

C. The Maturing Years

I am a California boy, raised in the culture and the climate of Southern California. Those of us who have been raised in the sun belt are conditioned to think of the seasons of the year as mostly the same. Although we are aware of the coming of spring, it is not a dramatic transition. Neither is it with the coming of fall or winter. Only the coming of summer is dramatic. The

53

seasons of the year are summer and not summer.

Several years ago my wife and I decided to take some time off between two conferences on the East Coast and drive through the region of our country that experiences the coming of autumn as marked by the changing of the leaves. I had always heard of fall but had never experienced it. Imagine our surprise when the colors of the leaves outperformed even our furthest expectations. I'll never forget the yellows, the reds, the golds, the browns, all blended into the landscape as if God had dropped His tray of paints, and they had spilled randomly onto the carpet of the earth.

But fall is not only beautiful in many parts of our country, it has another meaning as well. It marks the approach of winter. As such, it is a time of transition. Storm windows are brought out of the garage and attached to their winter resting place. Snow tires are rolled out of storage and positioned for the first storm. It is a time to get ready. Fall is beautiful for those of us who come to visit, but it is also a time of work for those who live there.

Then comes winter.

In the mind of a California boy, winter is romanticized. It is snow and snowmen. It is trees flocked with cotton and icicles hanging dramatically from the eves of houses. Children play happily, and fires burn warmly on the hearths of wintered America.

You can imagine my amazement when I had occasion to talk with an elderly man who had fled the frozen tumult of the upper Midwest for the comfort of Arizona. He was a snowbird in the vernacular of those of us from the sun belt states.

"Winter's hell, my friend. I wait to get away. I'm only glad I can afford it. I have friends who have to live there all year long, and during the winter they're miserable. Snow is slush more than it's snow. Your car rots from the salt on the streets, and you can't get warm all winter. I'd live here all year long if I could get my kids to move, but I can't. So I guess I'll just live part of the year up there and part of the year down here."

If I were to believe my snowbird friend, I would think that winter is all bad. But I'm reminded of another conversation I had with a farmer from one of the upper plains states.

54

"Winter can be pretty bad all right," he said. "But it's not all bad. Frankly, it's the time I recover from the rest of the year. It's the only time I have to sit and read and think. There's nothing else to do. Some of the time I repair my equipment, getting ready for the spring, but most of all I take the time to spend the evenings reading and thinking."

What a difference. I had walked away from my conversation with my snowbird friend saying to myself, "I'm glad I don't have to winter in the mess of the snow country." But in contrast, I walked away from my conversation with my farmer friend with a respect and with a bit of envy in my heart. I kind of wished I had more of what he had made for himself in winter.

I'm convinced that the Maturing Years are the fall and winter of our lives. Each time has its pluses, and each has its minuses. What makes them tolerable is our orientation. My California idealism is quickly brushed off as shallow and inappropriate by those who live through real winters, but the pessimism of the older gentleman in Arizona paints an altogether too dreary picture that would convince everyone never to venture north after the middle of October. Healthy reality lies somewhere in between.

6. The Empty Nest

The years of the Empty Nest are the fall of our lives. Like the fall they can be a time of great beauty, but they need to be a time of preparation as well.

The major task to be navigated during these years is the task of rediscovery. The empty nest begins with the launching of the first child into the Between Families stage, and is in full swing when the youngest child leaves home. What is left of the marriage when the children are grown and gone? Is the marriage positioned so as to allow for greater intimacy and freedom or is it fixed in such a way so as to be caught in the despair of loss and emptyness? Although most couples dread the thought of their last child leaving home, the research seems to indicate that many couples experience increased satisfaction during these years. Whatever direction it takes, it is a time of transition.

The opportunity for ministry by the Church to those in the Empty Nest Years includes providing the occasion for deepening friendships. One of the most significant research findings concerning these years has to do with the increase in the importance of friends. When the children leave, friends become family in many cases. There are no better friends than those who share a common commitment to Christ. However, friends, like family, take time. Because the leadership of the Church often comes from those in the Empty Nest Years, it is easy for the Church to become competitive and to preempt the time it takes to make and to keep good friends. One of the greatest ministries the Church has to those in the Empty Nest Years is to give them the space they need to rediscover their marriage and to enjoy their friends.

7. Retirement

Then comes winter. Beginning with retirement and ending with the death of the last spouse, Retirement-Years people face the major tasks of coping with a sense of uselessness, with the loss of health, with the loss of the spouse through death, and with preparation for and acceptance of one's own impending death. Too many aged persons end these years lonely and isolated from those who mean the most to them.

The Retirement Years can either be thought of as the end of the road or of the gaining of freedom to devote oneself to others and to the pursuits always left for another day. Finally there is time . . . but time for what?

The answer to this question is in fact the blueprint for the Church's ministry to those in the Retirement Years. Those who cope best with aging and the losses of the winter years seem to be those who have developed a system of mutual aid in which they are able to give aid and comfort to others and to receive aid and comfort as well. The system of mutual aid works best when it is intergenerational, that is, when it allows for there to be aid given and received across the generations. Secular research seems to support the Biblical idea of providing aid for "widows indeed" (I Tim. 5).

56

A system of mutual aid alleviates the problem of isolation as well. When there is need, there is reaching out, and the aging person's perception of self is not just that of a sponge but is that of usefulness. The same holds true for the predictable crisis having to do with the loss of one's spouse. It is a time for the Church to become the Church as it incarnates the comfort of the Holy Spirit in the lives of the bereaved.

Winter is not all that bad when you're not alone and when you're warm.

D. The Single Years

In terms of the model I am suggesting, the cluster called the Single Years is an anomaly. The "stages" of the Single Person and the Single Parent are not stages of development in the same way the other stages are. However, they must be included, not for the purpose of separating them from the other stages but for the purpose of drawing special attention to their unique situations.

The Single Years are unique in that they represent a group of people who are dissimilar from the mainstream of modern, Western culture. They are dissimilar only in that they have deviated from the norm—the nuclear family. The irony is that more and more they represent the norm if not the ideal. Two trends seem to illustrate what I mean.

Statistical trends as identified by the U.S. Bureau of the Census seem to predict that the majority of adults, that is more than 50 percent of adults, will have spent some significant time of their adult years as single, either as divorced or as widowed. Also, that same Census Bureau is predicting that more than 50 percent of all children who are now school age will have spent part of their school age years in a Single-Parent home. To be single, whether never married or formerly married, is a growing proportion of the population. The people of the Single Years must be taken into account if the Church is to be the Church in the twentieth century.

Where the singles are positioned in the life of the Church is not as important as whether or not their needs are met. I have served in churches which positioned them differently. In one church the singles were treated wholly separately and given classes of their own. They were not integrated into the other adult classes. In another church they were integrated into the regular adult structures of the church.

The problem with the first seems to be the unnecessary attention that is drawn to being single. Some people don't want to be treated differently. Also, it seems that in the case of many churches there are not enough singles to warrant a separate group of their own or, if there are enough, they are herded into one class irrespective of their diversity.

The problem with the second approach seems to be the likelihood that the single can be lost in the forest of married people and married concerns. It is all too easy to assume that the needs of the single person are being met if the needs of the age or stage group are being met. Not so.

One likely solution is a both/and solution. It seems to me that it is good for single people to be integrated into the life of the Church because they are normal just like everybody else. On the other hand, it seems appropriate that at some time in the calendar year they need to have time in which there is a focus on their particular needs. In healthy extended families, a single brother or a single aunt is not excluded just because they have never married or because they are divorced. On the contrary; they are integrated into the warp and woof of the family. But some discussions may seem irrelevant to them because they are single, and other discussions important for them may seem irrelevant to the married members of the family.

What I am arguing for is a special, highlighted status for the Single Person and the Single Parent in the Church. Rather than drinking last at the watering trough of the Church's resources, they need a place where they drink first. Only in that way can we be sure to be aware of and responsive to their needs.

8. Single Person

Some single young adults belong in the Between Families stage rather than in this stage. The Single Person in this "stage" is in his or her thirties or older and is divorced or widowed, or has never married. Research in this stage seems to indicate that at least two factors seem to surface which identify the major tasks.

The first factor has to do with their rootlessness. Many times they have never really settled down and established firm and continuing relationships. They can be habitually disconnected. The psychological result of this rootlessness is a strong, even desperate, need for belonging. How to be single and still feel like you belong to someone is the question.

The second factor is akin to the first. It has to do with feeling like a fifth wheel. It's different from not belonging. It is feeling like you don't really fit. It is being at parties and realizing that everybody there is paired up except you. It's trying to find someone to talk to about something other than kids. It's feeling different.

These two factors seem to me to provide the Church with its greatest opportunity for ministry to the Single Person. To begin with, if the Church is inclusive rather than exclusive, no one will feel left out. Everyone has the opportunity to belong. And secondly, an emphasis upon the Church as the new family of God will focus our attention upon relationships that are broader than marriage and parenting. Most churches are marriage-centered or child-centered, and as a result, the Single Person doesn't fit, being neither married nor a parent.

What I am suggesting is that the Church become kinship-centered, which allows for a simultaneous emphasis upon marriage and singleness. The greater bond is seen to be familial, especially defining the relationships as do the New Testament writers when they appeal to one another as brothers and sisters. I refer to this as an emphasis upon *siblial* relationships. We are not all married, and we all do not have children, but in Christ we are all brothers and sisters, not in a euphemistic sense of the word but in a familial sense. Anyone raised in a healthy family knows that one of the strongest bonds and senses of belonging is siblial. In fact, according to one secular writer, relationships between brothers and sisters seem to last the longest of all relationships and have the quality of greatest permanence.

Sports teams have chanted "we are family" and the world was impressed. The Church must do more than chant; we must become family and in becoming family the Single Person will both have a people to belong to and a place to fit.

9. Single Parent

When I graduated from seminary, I was initiated into the realities of life by the single adults in the church where I served. In particular, I remember the plight of the Single Parents and their needs. As a group of people I was touched by their situations partly because I was raised by a Single Parent, my father having died when I was seven. The combination of the two themes, their presenting problems and my personal history, has given me a special feeling for the Single Parent.

Now that I am older and have a family of my own, I have thought back on my own situation of growing up. My mother did the very best that she could do. But often I had needs as a young child, and later as an adolescent, that were more than my mother could meet by herself. I remember aching inside because of those needs, not knowing how to get them met and not having a system that was responsive to them. I was not a Christian, and we were not part of a church. Many of those needs have gone largely unmet, and much of the struggle of my adult years has been attempting to overcome that earlier deficit.

The Single Parent is asked to perform an impossible task: be both father and mother to the children. In many cases it is the mother who has that impossible responsibility. She must try to be the provider and the disciplinarian, as well as the care giver and the comforter.

(I am using traditional gender roles deliberately because, from the perspective of the child and from the perspective of most families, the father is still the dominant provider, and the mother is the prime care giver. Admittedly, this is changing. However, for purposes of this discussion, who does what is irrelevant. The point I am trying to make is that in the case of the Single Parent, usually a woman, she is required to do more than she can be expected to do. She is asked to work full-time usually

60

at a job that does not match the pay of her male counterpart. She must come home and be the arbiter of disputes, the cook, the laundry woman, and still have the energy to take her children on her lap and give them comfort when they hurt or attend their games when they play. What often results is that she becomes one or the other. Either she devotes herself to the provider role and lets the nurturant roles take a lesser importance, or she struggles resentfully with her provider role and tries desperately to be the care giver, giving her energy to it.)

The plight of the Single Parent provides the Church with one of its greatest opportunities to exhibit the servant qualities of Christ. Many Single Parent families suffer from inadequate or dysfunctional extended families. They are very alone. The opportunity for the Church is to become family to them.

A friend of mine was raised in the Mormon Church. He, too, was raised by a Single Parent. The difference in his case was that every week a man came by from the church to see how he was doing. At first, it was uncomfortable for him. As time went on he began to look forward to the visit. One of the questions that was always asked was whether or not the family was getting along financially. If they weren't, he would return to the leadership of the church, and immediately money was available to get them past their crisis. The church shared the provider role and expected the mother to continue in her care-giving functions.

Another illustration that seems relevant to me was the response of some of the men in the single adults class I taught when I first graduated from seminary. On one occasion it became known to the class that one of our members, a Single Parent, owned a home that had progressively deteriorated because of forced neglect. The members of the class organized a workday and attacked the problem of that neglected home. They painted, they hacked weeds, and they installed a new toilet. The day had an old-fashioned barn-raising quality to it.

At the end of the day I stood with the young woman whose home it was. Her voice filled with tears as feelings of gratitude threatened to overwhelm her. She couldn't say thank you enough. The class had become Christ for her that day, and the ministry of the Church had become real.

Not all Single Parents need their house repaired or help with the bills. What they often do need is a caring community tuned to their special needs. Like so many of us, they need their church to be *the* Church.

Concluding Remarks

My purpose in this chapter has been to suggest that the life cycle of the family provides a workable model for preventive, family-life education in the Church. I have gone further to suggest that no one, and no institution, is presently doing the job. The extended family system has been lost for many Americans. The schools are impotent and the government immobilized. The needs, however, are as great as ever.

The life cycle role changes come as predictably as they have for all of history. The difference is that each small nuclear family tries to cope with those role changes as if it were the first raft down the river. What has been created is a vacuum ready for the Church to fill. The information, skills, and the motivation to meet the changes in the family over time is the Church's ripest opportunity for ministry to the family today. But how?

First, the church that intends to launch a ministry to families need not begin with a full-orbed organization. What is important is to start somewhere.

Second, wherever you begin, someone needs to "own" the program; someone needs to have ultimate responsibility for its organization.

Third, small groups probably provide the most natural primary relationships for the discussion of these stage-related issues.

Fourth, the material is probably discussed best in informal settings—a living room, over dining room tables, on camping trips, etc.

Fifth, who can lead it? Who can best communicate these issues and develop the kind of relationships within which the nitty-gritty matters of life can be processed? We must seek a new kind of "expert." One who has experienced the realities of a particular stage and can speak with some kind of authority, even the authority of one who made mistakes. We must seize back the title of "expert" from those who have graduate degrees or those who have academic credentials. We may need a new breed of academically trained ministers to oversee such programs, but the experts for each step should be those people who have survived the realities of a particular stage and are motivated to provide leaders for the next generation. They need not be perfect and probably will be more effective if they lead from a position of vulnerability rather than a position of "having it all together." They need not be educated in a formal sense. However, they must be trained. It is the Biblical model of discipling, the older teaching the younger. We must look for those men and women in our congregations who can disciple best. They are the "experts."

6 Understanding 'Us'

A brief recapitulation of the material we've covered thus far might be helpful.

I have suggested that a necessary relationship exists between the Church's task of discipling and the family's natural place in the life of the person. Based upon this relationship, the Church needs to deliberately structure its ministry to involve the family and support the family in the task of discipling its own members.

Second, I have suggested that from the point of view of the family the task of discipling is very much akin to what is referred to as socialization in the secular literature, and this provides insight into how the task of discipling can be accomplished.

Third, I have suggested that the tasks of socialization or discipling change over time based upon which stage of the life cycle the family is in. Effective family ministry will therefore be different depending on where the family is in its personal history.

Now, I would like to introduce a fourth body of literature into our design for family ministry. It is the *systems approach* . . . to the family and to the Church. In the past the Church has approached its ministry primarily from the point of view of the individual and not from the point of view of the whole and the relationships that exist between its members. A systems approach lifts the interaction between the members of the whole to a place of prominence and places less emphasis upon the role of the individual. What results is a better understanding of the complexity of the human drama which is not simplistic, linear thinking. Linear thinking infers that if the first cause in a chain of relationships changes, then the rest of the relationships must change. For example (a pet peeve of mine), if we can get Dad to be the head of his home, then everything and everyone else under him will automatically fall into place. Such "chain-of-command" thinking neglects and even denies the interaction and the interrelationship that other members of the family have with each other and with God.

Linear thinking is deterministic. If the first cause fails, then the following relationships cannot help but fail. Somebody has to be blamed. Everyone else is off the hook.

64

On the other hand, in a systems approach in which interaction and feedback are requisite factors in understanding the family, choice and creativity are possible and even appropriate. Change is normal, and development is necessary. Therefore, if Dad is less than adequate in his job of being head of his family, it is appropriate for Mom or even others to step in and to creatively change the system. She is not caught in the dependent and deterministic position that says that she must get Dad to change before she can. Linear, causal thinking results in frustration and resentment on the part of the underlings who come to feel helpless and powerless. But systems thinking results in creative and positive change which allows anyone and everyone to become all that God means them to be.

In addition to challenging linear thinking and the determinism it fosters, a systems approach to the family provides suggestions for handling complexity rather than becoming overwhelmed by it. The modern world is very different from the world of the first century. Much of that difference lies in the complexity versus the simplicity of life-styles, comparing then with now. Because our world is so much more complex than the world of the first century, family life is more complex. How can the principles of Scripture be applied to this greater complexity?

The purpose of this chapter is to introduce you to a systems approach to the family which can integrate modern complexity into Biblical principles for effective family ministry.

The Importance of "And"

Sir Arthur Eddington, the famous British biologist, pioneered the application of modern systems theory to the field of biology. The following quote from Eddington demonstrates the special contribution systems theory makes to the study of any discipline:

> We often think that when we have completed our study of "one" we know all about "two" because "two" is the product of "one and one." We forget that we have to make a study of "and."

It is the understanding of "and" that makes the ministry to

humans so unique. God created male *and* female and in that act(s) He created the mystery we know as the family. You cannot understand a family or minister to that family until you understand the nature of "and" and the dynamics of relationships that "and" implies.

In fact, I would even go so far as to say that until you have fully ministered to humans in the significant relationships in their world, i.e., their "ands," you have not brought the full weight of the Word of God to bear on their human situation. As persons created in God's own image we are never to be thought of in isolation or as an island to ourselves. As God in the mystery of the Trinity is never in isolation, so man is never in isolation to himself but is to be thought of as a member of community. In that sense of the word, there is no such thing as an individual, only members of a whole.

The implications for the Church's ministry to families lie in the absolute necessity for the Church to address itself to the dimension of relationship. By this I don't mean an emphasis upon the gooey and syrupy tenets of so-called relational theology. What I am suggesting is an emphasis upon the dynamics of relationship and the communication skills needed to facilitate those relationships. Family ministry is therefore at the heart of the ministry of the church because it is in our families that we learn or fail to learn how to get along with one another, how to communicate or not communicate, etc.

Of all contemporary systems of knowledge, no other body of information has more to say to us than does modern systems theory in terms of the "how to's" of relationships and communication. A fully orbed ministry to the family must therefore include at least a basic understanding of the concept and nature of systems.

The Nature of Systems

When we talk about systems we are talking about a concept that has come to be useful in many varied and separate disciplines. Whether it is biology and the concept's usefulness in describing the interrelationships between the living organisms

66

and creatures that inhabit a coastal marsh or whether it is astronomy and the concept's usefulness in describing the inter-relationships that exist between the planets of our sun, the concept of system is broad and pervasive.

A system is anything that constitutes a cluster of highly in-terrelated parts, each responding to the other while at the same time somehow maintaining itself as a whole even when there is incessant internal change. The three parts of the definition are: *the parts are in relationship with one another; the whole is greater than the sum of the parts; and, the whole is able to continue and change in response to itself and to its environment.*

One example of a system is the Scripture's description of marriage. In the Book of Genesis we read, "Therefore a man leaves his father and his mother and cleaves to his wife, and they become one flesh" (Gen. 2:24, RSV). Marriage is more than a man plus a woman. Marriage is like a third person that is created between them, the "one flesh" that is greater than either one of them.

The importance of system becomes apparent when that "one flesh" relationship seeks help through counseling. Traditional individualistic psychology would assume that if you counsel the husband and then you counsel the wife, you have counseled the marriage. Nothing could be farther from the truth. You have not yet seen them when they are together, what they become when they are in relationship with one another. The nature of systems demands that you treat the whole as being more than the sum of the parts. Those of us who are married know that we often act and react differently when we are with our spouse than when we are with others. The mystery of marriage is the mys-tery of the interrelationship between the parts, that is, the sys-tem.

A second and marvelous example is the apostle Paul's de-scription of the Church in I Corinthians 12. Note the following verses in which Paul draws attention to the whole as well as the parts.

> For as the body is one, and hath many members, and
> all the members of that one body, being many, are

one body: so also is Christ (v. 12). For the body is not one member, but many (v. 14). But now are they many members, yet but one body (v. 20). And whether one member suffer, all the members suffer with it; or one member be honoured, all the members rejoice with it (v. 26).

The whole purpose of Paul's use of the metaphor of the human body is to draw attention to the fact that the whole is of greater importance than any one part and to draw attention to the dependency each part of the body has on the other parts. He draws attention to the relationship between the parts as being of utmost importance when in chapter 13 he expounds the importance of love. Love is a relationship word that defines the rules that govern how the parts are to relate to one another. Love is an "and" word. The Church, the Body of Christ, is a system to be governed by the fruit of the Spirit rather than by self-centered motives and aspirations.

This brings us to another important fact in understanding a system. Systems operate according to rules. Sometimes those rules are explicit and recognized by the members of the system and sometimes they are implicit. However, there are always rules. The task in understanding a system is not to gather data about the properties of the members of the system but to gather data about how the members interrelate with one another. For example, in the case of marriage counseling we focus not upon the internal psychological states of the married partners but upon their patterned responses to one another. These patterned responses we call communication. In fact, good communication in system terms is nothing more than increasing the useful exchange of information between the members. The exchange of information can be absent or it can be dysfunctional. When it is, poor communication results. When the exchange of information is appropriate, then good communication takes place, and the health of the system is preserved. The rules, whether functional or dysfunctional, determine the health or the disease of the system.

The last fact that must be discussed in order to understand the nature of systems is the property all human social systems demonstrate called *strategy*. People who live in complex human systems such as a family or a church share in the outcome of the system. Humans are participants in the functions of their systems rather than mere parts. The difference has to do with both intention and creativity. The members are collaborators. Let me give an example, again from counseling, that illustrates the concept of strategy.

Suppose a young teenager in a church complains to the youth leaders about his or her parents. The parents are "mean," "abusive," "impossible to live with," etc. If we engage in traditional individualistic, linear thinking, we will either join the teenager and think of the parents as being at fault or we will support the parents and think of the teenager as complaining unnecessarily, thus risking the alienation of the teenager.

Using a systems approach changes the way in which we come at the problem. The teenager and the parents are part of a family system and, therefore, share in the responsibility for the outcomes of the system. The family's strategy for some reason requires a conflict between the generations. Both the teenager and the parents for some unknown reason are collaborating, usually unconsciously, in the dysfunction. The hard work in the counseling process lies in uncovering the strategy that undergirds the family's action.

This concept of strategy suggests another move as well. It is that family strategies can be changed depending upon a change in the parts the members play one with another. If the strategy can be uncovered and exposed, then the members can provoke change in the system simply by refusing to play their part or by switching parts. The system always has room for contingencies. The difficulty lies in discovering the strategies and provoking the members to change their parts.

In the case of the alienated teenager, the family needs to face why the generations need to be angry with one another and then what any one person in the system can do to no longer collaborate in that alienation. The counselor must get someone to do something differently. If anyone changes, the system must change. Like the change in a mobile creates a change in its constituent parts, so a change on the part of one member of a system requires a change in the other members.

In summary, complex human systems such as families possess the ability to consciously or unconsciously collaborate in strategies that lead to helpful or hurtful outcomes. The members of the system share responsibility for those outcomes, and they can change their parts if they choose. The hard work comes in discovering the particulars of the strategies and in motivating the members to change their positions vis-á-vis the other members. They can vary the parts they play, and they can choose *not* to play. Facing their strategies and owning their outcomes becomes the agenda for the family's interaction and communication. What family strategies are particularly Christian? What "strategy" is the Church a part of? In what ways is the Church a collaborator in the family's outcomes? Tough questions but needful. We must ask ourselves these and more.

The Significance of Information

One rule in systems theory says that as any social system becomes more complex the kind of energy needed to run the system shifts from activity to information. Let me illustrate.

When we first married, my wife and I had a fairly simple life. There were just the two of us. As we got to know one another, we could anticipate the other's responses and adjust accordingly. Then came our first child. Life immediately became more complex. Once there was only one relationship to worry about, now there were three. I had to worry not only about Lucy but also about my relationship with the new baby and about Lucy's relationship with the baby. There was more to talk about and there was more to manage. The demands for more information between us became significantly greater.

Years later we were faced with a similar dilemma. We made the decision as a family to provide care for a foster son. There were the four of us in our family, and then came our new foster son. Although we knew better, we did not take fully into account just how much more complex our family had become with the addition of one more person. Soon after his coming we began to realize that we could not depend on the old patterns of communication that had served us so well for years. We had to do something more. Lucy decided after one very trying day that we needed to hold a family conference. That evening we sat around the table after dinner and took our temperature: What kind of week had each of us had? Then we each went around the table and told one another how we were feeling about the others in the family. Our emotions soon surfaced, and the lines of communication opened once again. We kept up that pattern of weekly communication until our foster son left 18 months later. Looking back, we realize that had we not increased our levels of communication we would have been completely immobilized and the pain would have been more than we could have handled. The axiom held true. As a social system becomes more complex either through the addition of another person or persons, or through the normal maturation of those in the system, the demand for information increases commensurate with the complexity.

According to systems theory, in order to be effective, a system must have the ability to process two kinds of information. First, the system must be able to gather and process information as to whether it is doing a good job and can stay the same. That kind of information is called negative feedback. Feedback is that process by which the system informs itself as to how it is doing both internally and externally. A family must be able to monitor its performance and know when it is functioning properly. The word negative is misleading. In system terms it does not mean negative in the sense of bad. It means negative in the sense that when you take a tuberculosis test and the results come back negative, you are all right. You can stay the way you are. Negative feedback means you don't have to change what you are doing and enter into some extensive medical treatment.

The second kind of information says when it is time to change. This latter kind of feedback is said to be positive, again not in a moral sense but in the sense that the system must adapt in order to survive. The ability of my wife to gather information about the pain in our family and to suggest methods for handling the pain is an illustration of positive feedback.

The key is in the family's ability to know whether it must

71

change or stay the same. Both kinds of feedback are necessary. The significance in terms of a church's family ministry lies in the family's need to be able to know when, why, and how to change.

Let me suggest an example. Suppose I have a 12-year-old daughter. She is my oldest child. From my friends in the community I hear all kinds of horror stories about what it's like to have your first teenager. I'm on my guard. When the hormones start flowing in my budding adolescent, I'm ready for anything. One day she's moody and testy. She seems to be aching for a fight. After a few days or even a few months, I grow weary of the tension that seems to surround our relationship and conclude that the worst has come.

"Whatever happened to that sweet little girl that used to live at our house?" I ask myself.

If my family is oriented toward change (i.e., positive feedback), I will probably try several ways to bridge the communicating gap that seems to have grown between us. However, if our family is oriented to staying the same (i.e., negative feedback) even when one of its members is changing, then I will probably try to force the situation and the relationships to remain the same. Probably the situation will go from bad to worse. Without ever meaning to foment rebellion, I can easily have a surly, rebellious teenager on my hands.

On the other hand, some parents are too ready to change. They panic. I remember talking with a young couple whose son had just cut school for the first time. As I listened to the parents, you would have thought that the boy was on the verge of juvenile delinquency. Their anxiety was running at a fever pitch. What they needed was a steadying hand to tell them to slow down and not to worry, which I did. Whereas in the first illustration the family system lacks the presence of positive feedback, in this second illustration the family lacks the presence of negative feedback. Their boy was okay. There was no need to panic. When they returned home, I later learned that they handled the situation simply and directly and let it go at that. The crisis passed and all was well.

Where do people learn how to change and why? Where do

they learn the rules of thumb that reassure them that they are doing fine and that they just need to hold the same course? Where does the family system learn the functions of both positive and negative feedback? They must learn it at the same place they learn about their stage in the life cycle, and they must learn it among a caring community which will reassure them when they needlessly panic or confront them when they must change. The Church must be a place where we are not only given information, such as from the pulpit, but it must also be a place where we learn how to gather information for and about ourselves. The Church must equip its people to handle the complexity of their lives by providing the necessary skills to cope. One of those most significant skills is the family's ability to process and handle information about itself and about its environment.

The Parts We Play

In terms of the basic nature of family systems, I suggest another set of concepts that can be of help in our understanding of how families work. The concepts are set forth in the excellent book by Kantor and Lehr, *Inside the Family*. These two researchers set out to discover how normal families relate to one another when they are together. Almost all of the studies about family life before Kantor and Lehr had to do with dysfunctional, hurting family systems. Very little, in fact, was known about how healthy families function.

In particular, they discovered that when family members are together they tend to adopt predictable parts like parts in a play. The part one is given or chooses (both are true) determines a great deal how the "ands" of the family work out in daily life. The parts exist when family systems are operative, and an understanding of the part one plays or is expected to play can be very helpful.

What I would like to do is to discuss each of these parts from the perspective of a family in the New Testament that Jesus loved—the family of Mary, Martha, and Lazarus. They, along with Judas, illustrate beautifully the "parts" of Kantor and Lehr.

73

The Mover

Martha is the mover in the family Jesus loved. She was the initiator. She got things going. She was an activist. One gets the feeling that Martha was on the bossy side and that she liked things to be organized. Movers are that way. They usually see themselves as the activity centers of the family. Often movers believe that little if anything will get done in the family unless they make it happen.

Movers are very important, because in truth little does get done in a family if someone is not there to initiate it. The problem for the mover is not who initiates what. It is the need to control and the need to choose what is best for others that creates the problem. Movers can engender resentment amongst the troops if they are not careful. They can either be drivers or leaders. Drivers push people along in front of them and characteristically provoke resistance and resentment in those who are expected to follow. Leaders on the other hand are just that. They lead. They go first and give those who are with them the freedom to follow. Leaders can be very persuasive, but ideally they are not coercive.

Some movers suffer from another fatal flaw in addition to the temptation to being drivers. They can, like Martha, become martyrs. Martha said, "Lord, dost thou not care that my sister hath left me to serve alone?" (Lk. 10:40.) Movers can become weary from much well doing and can feel very sorry for themselves. Movers can become complainers if their energies are not appreciated and if they are not followed.

However, movers have much good about them. They are active and not passive. They meet problems and people head-on. (Cf. John 11:20.) They are bold and dare to tell even the Lord what to do and how to do it. (Cf. John 11:21.)

What movers need to remember is that their initiative and action can never take the place of waiting for God, that is, allowing God to lead. Even though they tend to charge ahead of the pack, they need to remember to be patient and to allow others to be convinced for themselves and to choose for themselves.

74

Last of all, movers need to remember that they need others just as others need them. It is easy for movers to think only in terms of their initiative and not in terms of the energies of others. Movers, in order to be successful, can never be alone.

The Follower

The second part identified by Kantor and Lehr is that of the follower. Followers are especially appreciated by movers. Followers usually do what they are told. In fact, they need movers to tell them what to do. In the Scriptural narrative about Mary and Martha, Mary is the classic follower. She is seen sitting at Jesus' feet. She is responsive, and she is commended by Jesus for her responsiveness.

One of the problems for followers is the resentment they receive from the movers although movers need followers. Some movers are never pleased no matter what followers do.

The Bystander

According to Kantor and Lehr, many people in families play the part of the bystander. They are observers. They do not get involved. They are at the fringe of the action in the family. They are the onlookers who are present but not really a part of the heartbeat of the family.

In our narrative in Scripture, Lazarus is the bystander. Every time he is mentioned, he is passive, being acted upon rather than acting. In John 11 he has died and is the object of grief. He is the one who is called from the grave by Jesus. Bystanders, like Lazarus, are observers to the action around them. More often than not, life goes on and acts upon them.

The greatest problem for the bystander is the frustration they experience from the others in the family. It's tough if you're a mover to be married to a bystander. He or she just doesn't get involved. The responsibility for managing the family falls on the shoulders of someone other than the bystander. The bystander's major purpose is to avoid responsibility.

Also, another problem for the bystander is the constant pressure to get involved. In the case of Lazarus we are told in John 12 that even though he had been passive to the miracle of his resurrection, he still was the target of the wrath of the critics who sought to kill Jesus. He was a participant even though he was a bystander. He couldn't get away from it. Eventually even bystanders have to get involved.

The Resister

The fourth part in the model suggested by Kantor and Lehr is the resister. The resister is characterized by his position vis-à-vis the mover of the family. Opposition is the watchword. In some cases the resister performs a useful function in that he or she challenges the mover's inappropriate action. Not everything the mover wants is good. Sometimes it needs resistance.

However, the function of the resister in the family is to defeat the initiative of the mover. Often the follower is caught in the position of needing to choose who will be followed, the mover or the resister.

In our Scriptural narrative, Judas fits the role of the resister, although he takes his opposition to an extreme. In John 12 we are told that he criticizes the actions of Mary when she, as an act of worship, anoints the feet of Jesus. Like all resisters, Judas is known for his voting against rather than voting for, irrespective of what was being voted on. The classic resister is "against" for the sake of being against.

Implications

The implications of the Kantor and Lehr model go far beyond an application to the family. In any social system the tendency is for people to distribute themselves into one or more parts. In some systems we can play one part and in other systems we can play another. For example, it is not uncommon for a father to be a mover at work and a follower, or more typically, a bystander at home. However, when it comes to our families we characteristically tend to play the part we learned in our family of origin. Even though it is possible to change, it often is hard to do so.

76

The rub comes when the parts come together in less than ideal combinations. For example, you can imagine what happens when two movers in a system try to initiate action contrary to one another. Conflict results, and often one or the other becomes a resister. At those times the family becomes immobilized.

Again, some systems, especially families, begin without a mover when two followers marry. In those cases, no one is there to run the ship. No one is at the helm. Usually the children become the movers, and the family becomes extremely child-centered. Effective social systems need to identify appropriate parts for the persons who constitute the system.

In light of the parts suggested by Kantor and Lehr, one of the struggles for the contemporary church is the appropriate roles for both males and females in the family. Frankly, it is my opinion that God does not intend all males to be movers and all females to be followers even though that seems to be the way we have come to interpret the issue of headship in the Christian family. Instead of predetermining the roles of the spouses based upon the false issues of gender, we need to help them come to some agreement as to the rules they will use in determining their roles. Some families are better off with mom as the mover and dad as the follower. What is of greater importance is, who serves?

The Servant

One of the most powerful "and" words in all of Scripture is the word *servant*. The nature of the word defines the relationship that is to exist between two or more Christians. As Christ became a bond slave for us, so are we to become bond slaves for one another. We are not to seek only our own interests but are to seek the interests of others. It seems to me that the genius of the first-century church was its willingness to lay aside traditional roles and to serve one another. Paul's exhortation was that in Christ "There is neither Jew nor Greek, there is neither bond nor free, there is neither male nor female: for we are all one in Christ Jesus" (Gal. 3:28). The Church is to operate according to some other principle.

Even though the parts people play in the human drama of the family sometimes can lead to conflict, the rule for the Christian is to serve in love. All other roles are insignificant in comparison with that overarching responsibility. Whether we are movers, followers, bystanders, or resisters, the mandate for us all is to be willing to play the most important part of all, that of servant.

Conclusion

What have I suggested in this chapter? First of all, I am suggesting that the Scripture does place and therefore the Church must place an emphasis upon relationships in order for its people to be whole. I am suggesting that the emphasis upon relationships needs to be more than the fuzziness of the past. It needs to be an emphasis that is informed by the way in which people function; that is, they live and work in patterned ways, they live in systems. Modern systems theory is the most illuminating way to understand human relationships today. It has informed us in the area of management, in the hard sciences, and in the soft sciences. And it can inform the Church.

I am also suggesting that a systems approach to family ministries in the Church will highlight the importance of communication and the exchange of information as a critical skill in the life of the family. Family ministries in the Church can and must facilitate the skills and the abilities of persons in families to interact with one another constructively and effectively.

Last of all, I am suggesting that when we come together in families we do so according to predictable roles or parts. We cannot avoid playing those parts. What is needed is an understanding of the parts we play and a commitment to allow the role or part of servant to govern all that we do. The Holy Spirit speaking through the inspired writers of Scripture has defined for us the relationship rules that are to be given priority. It is not a matter of who decides, who obeys, or who submits. The greater issue is how we relate to one another and how we decide how we will relate. In that sense, the Scripture is God's handbook for the "ands" in our lives.

7

Understanding 'You and Me'

The same systems literature that informs us about the importance of relationships and the importance of the useful exchange of information in complex relationships also informs us of the motivations of the members of the system. These motivations form the dynamic that energizes movement within the family system. If we can identify why members do what they do, then we can structure appropriate materials and opportunities for interaction that facilitate growth in terms of these often hidden motivations.

All too often our motivations are hidden, not operating at the conscious level. What is needed is a plan that brings these motivations to the surface, one that asks the family to place its agendas out on top of the table. Then we need a systematic means whereby we meet together as the Church in a caring community and face the implications of our individual agendas as they affect our families. What are those agendas, and what are their implications for family living?

What do we need?

In their book *Inside the Family*, Kantor and Lehr have identified three major motivations or goals that seem to energize the person in his or her actions in the family and toward the environment. These goals or targets as they are called are *affect, power* and *meaning.* For purposes of our discussion let's look at them, pull them apart, and analyze what each means in terms of family ministry.

To begin with, it is important to understand that we all need or want all three of the goals at some time or another. The issue is not that we need one or the other but which target seems characteristically to animate us the most. All are there in varying degrees but usually only one is most important. The trick is to find out which is most important. Now, what are these goals?

Affect

The first goal is that of *affect.* Kantor and Lehr assign a somewhat unique meaning to the word which conjures up the idea of affection. It is meant to mean that and more. Affect has two basic dimensions. The first is the need for intimacy which can be thought of as the need for mutual emotional closeness among peers. Although affect often involves physical intimacy, that is not the main focus of the need. The main focus of intimacy is upon the exchange at the emotional level between two people who are equals.

The second dimension of the word affect is that of *nurturance*. Nurturance is the exchange of emotional support and encouragement sometimes between peers but more often between generations such as between parent and child. It is the care and comfort given to others because of *their* need and only secondarily because of one's own need. There is, however, an interaction effect. Nurturance is often given by those who need to give and who receive strokes for giving.

The difference between intimacy and nurturance is significant to note in terms of the family system. If people are motivated to seek intimacy in a family, they will send out signals. They will make demands for sharing. They often will just want to talk for the sake of talking. They will be encouraged when there is openness and vulnerability and distressed when there is secretiveness and defensiveness. The person who is seeking affect at the level of intimacy is seeking a relationship with a peer that will foster mutual emotional closeness and warmth.

In contrast, a person who is seeking affect at the level of nurturance is often seeking either care or comfort or a combination of both. For example, when my child skins her knee and comes home crying, she needs me as her parent to clean her knee up, doctor it, and then hold her in my arms and comfort her because she is hurting. The intimate relationship can be thought of as being represented by an arrow with a head at both ends where the relationship of nurturance can be represented by an arrow with a head only on one end. Intimacy is reciprocal. Nurturance is usually unidirectional.

Affect can be thought of as the heart of the family system. It is the need in all of us to love and be loved. As such it animates all of us to a greater or lesser degree. It also determines how family

80

members join and separate from one another.

Let me illustrate.

Earlier in this book I suggested that there is a kind of emotional stickiness to a family, that which ties or binds us together. In unhealthy families that stickiness is so powerful that members either are unable to leave the family and remain bound to it even when they are adults, or they are forced to yank free from it, thus severing relationships with the other members of the system. In contrast, healthy families seem to be able to allow their members to leave when it is time to go and to bless them for it. Later, the emancipated members are free to come and to go with ease.

Right at the heart of the issue of joining and leaving is the need for affect. Often, for example, a mother will need to hold onto her children because of her need to give nurturance, and the children will need to stay bound to her because of their need to receive nurturance.

Whatever the reasons, there are those of us who strongly, even desperately, need and seek affect. It is the issue that pushes us into relationships with others, and it is that which sometimes causes us to hold too tightly to others.

Power

The second goal or target that is common in families is *power*. There are many ways to define power, but in terms of family systems the definition is somewhat unique. Power is the freedom to decide for yourself what it is that you want, and the ability to secure it.

Where affect defines the horizontal axis of the family, power defines the vertical. Affect is the "heart," and power is the "muscle." It is very similar to the old adage of the pecking order.

I never fully understood the nature of a pecking order until my wife started raising canaries. One day she introduced a young cock to the aviary. Immediately the young birds began to fly toward the newcomer and attempted to startle him. He would fly from one side of the aviary to the other only to be charged again. Finally, as we watched, he flew to the floor of the cage to eat. At that moment what appeared to be the dominant male flew from one of the upper perches and charged head-on into the younger bird. Startled, the younger bird flew away. The aviary had a pecking order. The dominant ate first, and then those who were subordinate ate second, right on down the list until the poor bird who was last in line had to hope that something was left.

Power in family systems is like that pecking order. Those who have the power can decide what they want, and they have the ability to get it. Those who are less powerful have to wait in line. Sometimes they have to forgo what it is they want because those who are more powerful have preempted their choice.

The ideal, of course, is a balance in which each member in the family is given the freedom to gain access to the goals he or she seeks. In the day-to-day living of families it's not that easy. At least it's not been easy for our family.

I must admit that in terms of the pecking order of our family, I'm usually the one who has decided what he wants and has the ability to get it.

I remember one occasion just a few years ago. I decided that I wanted to move the family because I was tired of the long commute on the freeway between where I worked and where we lived. I had taken a teaching job with the understanding of my family that I would adjust to the travel. The commute was 45 miles one way, and depending on the traffic, I could make it home in an hour to an hour and a half. After a year, I was sick and tired of driving. I wanted to move closer to the school where I was teaching.

As is her habit, Lucy was willing to consider the change. She has been supportive of me, and even when she really doesn't want to, she has uprooted herself and followed me to where I wanted to go. In terms of the pecking order, she has been willing to subordinate herself to me. She is the paragon of a team player.

In terms of the children, I just assumed that they would naturally fit in. They had in the past, and my habit was not to worry too much about them. That was my first mistake. I took them for granted.

Having made the decision to move, we thought it best to communicate with the kids about the decision. The problem was that Sheryl, our oldest, was on a three-week trip to Europe with her grandmother. Because our family doesn't believe in secrets, I called Sheryl from Los Angeles to West Germany. Her voice on the other end of the phone was remarkably clear. I told her of our decision and of our intention to begin immediately looking for another house. I knew she would be upset, but I didn't anticipate the degree. When we hung up the phone, I could tell that she was hurting. She was a sophomore in high school, and she loved her school and her friends. She really wanted to stay where we were and to graduate from her very own school with her very own friends. But the thought of two more years of commuting was more than I could handle.

We began looking for a house near where I taught. Three weeks later we still had not found one. It seemed as if the doors had all closed. Still, I wanted to move. When Sheryl came home from Europe, I can remember the look on her face when she walked off the plane. She was glad to see us, but her eyes were filled with pain. Soon after she approached Lucy and me with a suggestion. It took the form of a bargain. The deal was that if I would be willing to commute for one more year, she would be willing to double up on her classes and attempt to graduate a year early. My first impulse was to say no because it would be too hard on her. But Lucy, who at times like these is often much wiser than I, suggested that we find out if it were possible.

The next day Sheryl and I met with the vice-principal of her high school. Sheryl outlined her proposal, and the administrator sat in his chair dumbfounded.

"Yes, it would be possible," he said. "But do you realize what you're getting into? First, you would have to take seven classes a semester. Second, you are a cheerleader and would have to come to school at 7:30 a.m. every morning for practice. You're also the captain of the girls' gymnastic team, and you have to practice until 5:00 p.m. every day. And on top of all of that, you will need to go to a local hospital on Monday and Wednesday evenings from 6:00 until 10:00 p.m. for an extended education experience."

"Do you think you can do it?" he asked. I both wondered and worried.

"Well, I really do want to graduate from my school, and I don't want Daddy to have to commute for two years. If he's willing to do what he's doing, then I'm willing to give it a try."

As we walked out of the vice-principal's office, I didn't know why, but I knew that what had just happened was very good. Later, as Lucy and I talked, I realized for the first time that we had turned the pecking order upside down, at least in terms of Sheryl's needs. It was one of the first times that I had been willing to put aside my supposed "right" to take care of my needs first simply because I was the one at the top of the pecking order.

When the year was over, we all looked back with amazement. I had survived my commute. Sheryl had not only survived, but she graduated with the best grades that year that she had ever gotten in high school. We found a house that we really liked, and, most significantly, when it came time to move, Sheryl was fully invested in the move and willing to go.

Best of all, I had to look my needs for power full in the face. I had always assumed that my needs came first. The trouble was that I easily bundled up my needs in "God's will" wrapping paper, and tied them with my "ministry" goals ribbon. The others in my family were expected to go along or somehow be out of God's will.

I really don't know how I'll face the next challenge to my power needs, but I do know that my assumptions for all of those years proved false, and my fears were unfounded. It is possible for a family to operate on something other than a "Father eats first" basis. I'm convinced that it's not only possible but also Scriptural. The hard work is the details.

Meaning

The third goal or target that motivates members in families is the goal of *meaning*. Whereas affect is the heart of the family system, and power is the muscle, meaning is the mind. Meaning is very close to the idea of identity, except that in family system terms, it is to be taken more broadly.

Meaning is the family's development and maintenance of its sense of self as a living whole. Like individuals, families develop self-concepts about who they are in contrast to who the others are in the world out there. For example, in this country when a woman marries, she is expected to take her husband's name and drop her own family name. That's just assumed to be appropriate. But many women suffer a deep sense of loss when they are asked to jettison their last name for a new one. What is it that they lose? It is their sense of family identity or the sense of meaning they derived from their family of origin.

Every healthy family has a sense of "who we are" and a sense of "who they are." The sense of "who we are" is the family's sense of meaning.

I remember when we first married, I walked into a family buzz saw that took me several years to figure out. That first year of our marriage we ate two Thanksgiving dinners, and we ate two Christmas dinners. Both of our families of origin wanted to incorporate us into their sense of who they were. I had married Lucy, and she had married me, but we were not yet thought of as a family to ourselves. Each family of origin wanted to keep us for their own, to maintain their family meaning. The problem was, how would we establish a sense of our own family? The answer came in two stages. First of all we moved to Texas and were 1,500 miles away from both of our families. I'm reminded of the premarital advice we received from the pastor who married us. He told us that we'd be smart if we lived at least a half day's buggy ride from our parents. It was the same advice given newlyweds at the turn of the century. The thought was to keep parents from intruding and to make it difficult to run home to Momma.

The second part of our answer was the birth of our first child. Somehow when we became parents, we also became a family. I can't explain it, but the change was very real. We expected to be treated as a separate and distinct unit.

Several years later we returned to live and minister in the area where we both grew up. Except for a few minor incidents, our families never again got their feelings hurt because we wanted to celebrate our own holidays or have our own traditions to enhance our own sense of family meaning. The something more we gained with the birth of our children is the sense of meaning that Kantor and Lehr talk about.

Affect, power, and meaning: three goals that people in families want, need, and spend energy seeking. But how? You will remember that earlier I talked about the strategies that family systems create for themselves. In healthy families those strategies coalesce in such a way that the individual members of the family are able to achieve their goals while supporting the goals of the other members of the family. The greater question is how is that accomplished? What do they do and how do they do it? The answer to these questions lies in a discussion of the means that families use to achieve their goals.

What we use to get what we need

Families need very little in the way of resources to help their members achieve what they want. According to Kantor and Lehr, the family has only three means or media which they manipulate in order to meet those needs. These means are *space, time,* and *energy.* In some ways it's very simple. The pulsing of the family in terms of the motivations of each can be understood not only in terms of the goals they seek but also in terms of the means they use. Space, time, and energy. Just three, but very significant.

Space

The first commodity the family uses to meet its need is that of *space.* Space is just what the word implies. It is the living environment of the family. There are two kinds of space—inside space and outside space. The first, inside space, is equivalent to the space that is represented by the living quarters of the family. How a family divides its living space tells you something about the people who live there.

Two examples point out the nature of inside space in the family. The first would be what happens when two siblings share a room. Any parent who has coped with the ruminations and conflicts that arise when two youngsters share a room knows what I'm talking about. Usually somewhere down the middle of the room is an invisible line. It is a boundary that marks the borders of the person's territory. Every so often someone will stray over the border, and an incident will occur.

"He's making a mess on my side of the room." Or, "When she rearranged the room she left me no place to put my things." The illustrations go on and on. Everyone has a sense of personal territory.

A second illustration would be the tension that often surfaces when an adolescent decides that his or her room is off limits to everyone else in the family, especially Mom. Up until that time Mom has usually had unrestricted access to the room. She has cleaned, straightened, decorated, cajoled, and basically controlled the space. Suddenly she is barred from the room by the edict of a wet-behind-the-ears kid who has decided that Mom is too pushy, too bossy, and too intrusive. Who is to control the space? What is to be hung on the walls? What posters will be considered appropriate? Whose standards for cleanliness are to be followed?

The illustration points up how the various needs of the members of the family come into conflict with one another. Perhaps Mom has the power need to control the lives of her children, and she doesn't intend to let that control be relinquished to some smart-mouthed kid. On the other hand, the adolescent has the need to assert his or her own sense of identity or meaning. "The other kids have posters on their walls," or "their mothers knock on the door before they come in rather than walking in unannounced." The collision is between two needs or goals, and the arena is inside space.

The second kind of space, outside space, provokes the same kind of interaction. Outside space is everywhere else the members in the family go beyond the borders of their home. When a little kid begins to ride his or her tricycle on the sidewalk, the parents usually set some kind of limits to the child's outside space.

"Don't go any farther than the corner. And whatever you do,

don't ride your tricycle in the street." The parents are setting boundaries for the child in terms of outside space.

When the child begins to mature, the boundaries are expanded, the parents have begun to relinquish control of outside space to the youngster. Then comes the first major test: 16 years old and the first driver's license. Every culture, whether it is the bushmen of Australia or the nomadic tribes of the Southern Sahara, has what is referred to by anthropologists as a rite of passage. A rite of passage marks the passage of a young person from childhood to the privileges of adulthood. I'm convinced that the granting of the driver's license in our culture has that kind of meaning attached to it in the minds of teenagers. It marks a time of liberation from the constraints of the parents' sense of outside space and the opportunity for adolescents to establish their own sense of self. The arena chosen to do this is outside space.

The tragedy occurs when, again, outside space becomes the media in which the issues of affect, power, and meaning are worked out inappropriately.

Take, for example, the teenager who tells his parents that he's going over to his friend's house and then out to a movie. The parents agree because his stated use of outside space is consistent with their rules for the family (i.e., family meaning). At 2:00 a.m. they receive a call from the local police. Would they come down to the station and pick up their boy? He has been arrested at a rock concert in a nearby town and was found to be in possession of marijuana. In deep shock they drive to the police station. They sign the papers for his release and start the long ride home. Silence fills the car. Anger and defensiveness seethe beneath the surface. When they finally arrive home in the privacy of their living room, chaos breaks out. Dad screams, Mom cries, and the boy responds angrily. Who would ever have thought that a "fine Christian family" would ever be found in such a position? The answer is that we all experience the same dilemma—some to a greater and some to a lesser degree. What is taking place is the conflict between the needs of the members of the family. The conflict is mediated in terms of the boundaries, in this case, of outside space. Perhaps Dad's concern is for power. He's not about to have a son of his throw his life away as a no-account. Perhaps Mom's concern is for affect. She's losing the closeness between herself and the boy. She can remember when he used to come home from school and sit at the kitchen table and tell her all about his day. He would talk, it seemed, for hours. In contrast to their needs is the boy's own need for power or for individual meaning. He's tired of Dad always telling him what to do and where to go, and he's fed up with Mom's endless questions. He just wants to be left alone.

Every family has crises. What is more tragic even than the crises is the fact that too few families have the communication skills needed to resolve the crises. Even fewer have ever thought through the reasons why they do what they do. Their needs operate at the unconscious level and they seem bound to repeat the mistakes of the past. Their need provides the church with one of its priceless opportunities for ministry: to help families identify their system's goals, and to learn how to openly communicate them to one another.

Time

In addition to space, the family has use of a second commodity which it uses to meet its needs. It is the commodity of time. Time, according to Kantor and Lehr, takes the form of both *clock time* and *calendar time*. Clock time has reference to the hours of the day. Calendar time has reference to the weeks and months of the year. Time becomes an object that is used by the members of the family to meet the goals they seek.

In terms of clock time, think in terms of a watch. It may be that most of the members of the family own watches and they all can tell time. However, usually one person in the family wears the family's watch, the one who determines when things happen.

I'm convinced, for example, that the problem many families have with being on time, whether it is to school, to church, or anywhere, is a problem of someone's resistance to the way in which the family's watch is being worn. In such cases clock time becomes the arena in which the issue of power or control is expressed.

The same holds true with the calendar. Open conflict often erupts when someone in the family decides that he or she is being left out of the decisions regarding the family's calendar. *When* we do what we do can become an important issue. If it does, it usually means that something else is going on, and the calendar is only the focus of the frustration. The greater issue is to get at the needs that underlie the conflict about the watch or the calendar.

Take, for example, the cry of many family members for someone "to take time with me." What are they saying? Probably they are saying that they have affect needs either for intimacy or for nurturance and the failure to spend time, usually clock time, is taken to mean that they are not important. Often just spending "time" is more important than what is done during the time.

I remember, for instance, a friend of mine who remarked one day that he was glad that he was in the habit of sitting on his daughter's bed at night before she went to sleep. From the time she was a young child, it was his job to tuck the kids in at night and to talk and pray with them before they went to sleep. Years later he had ceased sitting on their bedside every night because they were older, and it didn't seem appropriate. However, on one occasion, as he said good night to his teenage daughter, she asked if he would stay and talk for a minute. It felt natural to take the time and talk. She began to tell him of the problems she was having with her boyfriend. She thought she was in love with him but didn't know how to tell. As the conversation progressed, they were able to talk about the physical attraction that existed between the young couple and how to deal with that part of the relationship. By the time the conversation ended she reached up, hugged her father, and thanked him for listening to her.

As he recounted the experience to me, he was struck with the importance of the earlier times he had sat on the edge of the bed and listened to what seemed to be some of the most irrelevant issues and events in a young child's life. He recalled how he was tempted to cut his daughter off because he had "more important" things to do. But he hadn't. He sat and listened. Later, the time he had spent was like money in the bank. When his daughter moved beyond the irrelevant to the very important, their nurturant relationship was in place, and the commodity of clock time had been well invested. The lesson for us all is that good communication never takes place in a vacuum. It takes place in the context of relationships that have experienced the investment of both clock and calendar time. Time is often much more important than we realize. It's altogether too easy to take it for granted and to underestimate it as a significant dimension in the lives of those we love.

Energy

The third commodity that a family uses to meet its needs is the commodity of *energy*. Energy, according to Kantor and Lehr, comes in two categories as well. It is either kinetic or it is static. Kinetic energy is equal to the activity of the family. It is "what we do," with the emphasis upon the doing. Static energy, in contrast, is energy at rest. It is equal to the way in which the family gathers strength when it rests.

Again, an example for each might be helpful. Space can be thought of as the *where* we do what we do. Time is the *when* we do what we do. And energy is the *what* we do when we do it.

I remember a pastor's son who expressed the pain of his adolescent years in terms of where the family was forced to spend their vacations. Because the father liked to golf (i.e., energy), the family was required to spend two weeks of every year at a plush golf resort while the father enjoyed himself on the links every day. The problem was that there was very little for teenagers to do. They could lay in the sun by the pool, or they could go for a walk, or they could stay in the condominium and watch television. After the first few days the boy would hole up in front of the TV, whiling away his time and becoming increasingly resentful. Finally, when he was 16, he refused to go on vacation with his parents. They were crestfallen and labeled his resistance as rebellion. At the time he was unable to put his frustration into words, and a gulf was fixed between him and his father. Rather than find a solution that was good for everybody concerned, their family played a no-win game where someone

91

had to lose. In the end the loser was their relationship. Only later in his adult years was he able to see that his father was first in the pecking order of the family and chose to exercise that control in the choice of the family's vacation. Energy, that is the *what* a family does, always tilted to the father's benefit.

In contrast, a former teacher of mine had the policy that a family vacation belonged to the whole family. Everybody had a right to have input into the decision. One summer it was decided that each person in the family could decide what the family would do for one week of their vacation. The youngest son chose to go to amusement parks and to ball games, none of which was of interest to the rest of the famiy. But because it was fair, the family members went together and had a good time. The goodness of the experience was in the being together. The matter of *what* they did was only a commodity to be appropriately distributed according to each one's need.

Static energy, on the other hand, has to do with how a family gathers energy or recoups energy that has waned. Very simply put, what does a family do when it is at rest? Are there some activities that are allowed, such as reading or watching TV and others that are not, such as reading comic books or listening to rock music? The leisure pursuits of the family can become as much a problem as can the kinetic pursuits.

What family members *do* with their time becomes the arena in which the issues of affect, power, and meaning are processed and are either handled well or are handled poorly.

What we must do for one another

It is one thing to recognize that members of a family have different goals and use different commodities to meet those goals. It is another thing to do something about it. I'm convinced that one of the peculiar geniuses of Christianity is its ability as taught in Scripture to adapt appropriately to individual, family, and churchly needs. The great question for us all is *how?*

I have come to regard the teaching of the apostle Paul in Philippians 2:3, 4, and the example of the emptying of Jesus Christ described in verses five through eight, as paramount in the ability of the individual to fit with his family and the family to fit with the Church. Three relationship rules seem to me to be important.

The Rule of the Servant

The first is the *rule of the servant*. In verse three Paul enjoins each of us never to act from a motive of selfishness or from a motive of conceit. From the perspective of the family system material presented previously, selfishness would be considered as the assumption on the part of one member or another that the commodities of space, time, and energy automatically belong to them rather than belong to the family as a whole. Selfishness is "me first." Conceit would be the assumption that I choose for you as to how you use your space, spend your time, or what you do with your energy. Conceit is, "I know what's best for you."

The difficulty in a family is to avoid both of these extremes. Even though parents are given responsibility for their children and many times that responsibility requires definite control, still the Scriptural mandate is to act toward another in light of what you know to be their best interests.

The Rule of Assertiveness

That brings us to the second rule. It is the *rule of assertiveness*. You will note that Paul counsels us in verse four to act *not only* in terms of our own interests. Paul assumes that everyone has interests of his or her own. Some of us forget this, especially in families. Much damage is done when someone in a family is passive in expressing his own interests and habitually fails to say what it is that he wants or needs. It is acceptable for us to assert our own interests. It is appropriate for us to say what it is that we need or want. From this perspective the Church suffers as much from passivity as it does from selfishness. Unfortunately, there are many of us who never speak up. We are easily lost in the process.

93

The Rule of Equity

The third rule is the *rule of equity*. Again, Paul counsels us to look after the interests of others as well as our own. The emphasis is upon relationships having an implicit fairness to them. It is never right for a relationship to become inequitable, even though it may become unequal at times. The difference is between the terms equity and equal. The latter term connotes a sense of space being divided up into equal proportions, time into equal portions, and energy into equal shares. Unfortunately, it's neither possible to live life that way, nor is it wise. In the normal push and pull of life there are times when things can't be equal or even shouldn't be equal. An infant demands much more time than does an older child. The situation requires different strategies for each member. What is needed is a sense of equity. That is, no one in the family ever gets lost. Members can expect that every time it will work out fairly, if not equally.

I'm sure we've all heard the words, "it's just not fair," at one time or another. At our house we heard the words at a most unusual time and from the person in our family who is most likely to get lost in the family system. It was Shannon, our youngest child.

Because of the demands on my time, through the years we have sat down as a family and coordinated our calendar three months at a time. On one particular occasion we went around the dinner table, each one notifying the others about scheduled events. At the end of the exercise, Shannon sat, arms folded, with a scowl on her seven-year-old face.

"What's wrong, Shannon?" we all asked.

"When are we going to do something that I want to do?" was her strident reply. Her frustration was barely beneath the surface.

Sheepishly we looked at our calendar only to see that everybody in the family had something scheduled which required everyone's participation except Shannon. She was involved with everyone else, and we were involved with each other, but nothing required us to focus on Shannon.

"What would you like to do?" I asked.

"Well, I think I'd like to go to Universal Studios." At the mention of the name I cringed. Universal Studios is a family amusement park in Southern California that highlights the film and TV industry, and which has become a major tourist attraction in the area. I could think of nowhere else that I would less want to go. I can remember looking around the table only to be met with neutral stares from the others who understood my antipathy to such places.

My eyes passed to my calendar only to see that Washington's birthday was open. It was a free day. What else could we do? So we agreed, and the family began to make plans to go to Universal Studios.

When the day arrived, we clambered into our car and took off. The prospects of TV shows were swirling in Shannon's head, but the prospect of monstrous crowds were swirling in mine. When we arrived, I was right. Half of Southern California had come to Universal Studios, and they were all standing in line in front of us. Inch by terrible inch we made our way to the head of the line to be ushered into the Studio only to be faced with another massive line. The day had a dreadful beginning.

As the tour progressed Shannon became more and more animated, and the rest of us became more and more disinterested. She was having the time of her life. I was struggling. Hours later the day ended, and we pushed our way to the parking lot. As I walked along thinking of my aching feet and the prospect of the ride home through traffic, Shannon ran around in front of me and in her typical fashion flung herself up into my arms.

"Daddy, this has been one of the best days I've ever had in all of my life." With that she gave me a big kiss, hugged me, and skipped happily toward the car.

I can remember the look on our faces, and I can remember the chastisement of the Holy Spirit in my heart.

"Look not only after your own interests, but also after the interests of others," I had read, but I don't think I had ever really faced what the words meant. Those of us who live in the Guernsey family are responsible to look after the interests of the other person before we look after our own. Because I was positioned at the top of the pecking order, it was natural for me to take care of myself and then to look after the others. It was natural for them to do the same. Unfortunately, the little girl at the bottom too often gets lost in the shuffle, especially when it came to my time and attention. The years since that time have been taken up trying as a family to live consistently with Philippians 2:3, 4.

I'm convinced that every family has a Shannon—that person who is the last in line, the quiet one who never asserts his or her own way, the one who gets along and seems always to fit in. What makes us Christian in terms of our relationships is the commitment on the part of us all, especially those of us at the top of the pecking order, to see to it the Shannons of our family have their needs met. That's the least we must do for one another. When we do, we open ourselves up to one another and increase the likelihood that we will understand one another. Only then can we begin to "Let this mind be in you, which was also in Christ Jesus" (vs. 5).

8
A Family
Of Families

What has been suggested thus far pertains to the dynamics that characterize the individual family. Families are systems of interacting persons who maintain relationships with one another based upon the needs they have and their access to the resources that are available to the family. Those resources can be thought of as commodities which are distributed within the family. What is important for our understanding of families and the mission of the Church are a family's rules that govern the distribution of those resources. The Church should interpret the Scripture which relates to those rules.

The Church must be more conscious of the Scriptures that govern the relationships between family members than it has been in the past. Rather than becoming preoccupied with an endless search for the "absolute truth" about a particular role and programs that support that role, the Church must focus on two, more important questions: How does a particular role as defined in the Scripture fit in today's world in terms of its meaning? And, what are the relationship rules in Scripture that govern the interaction of that role with other roles in the family?

The answer to these questions will provide us with a working definition of any role in terms of the here and now and will give us a hermeneutical basis for interpreting the meaning of Scripture for today. Said in another way, we are to occupy ourselves with what the Scripture says about the "ands" in our present-day world. The specifics of the roles may change depending upon the course of history and upon the nature of a particular culture. What does not change is the Scriptural teaching about how we are to live with one another. Scripture tells us very little about the realities of our modern technological world, but it does tell us how we, as members of the Church and the family, are to relate to one another. Thus, the Scripture speaks to a man in a primitive culture in which the role of father is carried out, not by the biological father, but by the mother's oldest brother. Whatever father means in that culture is to be governed by the Scriptures in order to meet the child's need for wisdom, discipline, and supportive love. In the same way, the Scripture speaks to the modern employer who is to treat his employees with dignity even though the idea of employer was totally foreign to the writers of Scripture who were accustomed to the realities of the master/slave relationship. We are again reminded of the importance of "and."

Having said all of this, we move now to a discussion about the Church. If the above is true, there are enormous implications in terms of the mission of the Church. Each church must see itself in a new way, as a family of families. Such a redefinition requires a new role for the Church, a new role for the pastor, and a new role for the laity—roles which are intentionally flexible and open.

A New Role for the Church

The last half of the twentieth century has become an era of heightened individualism. We are told to look out for number one, and to grab all of the gusto we can get because we only go around once in life. Ours is an individualistic and narcissistic age. The influence of these two cultural forces is far greater than we might realize. Within a year most pastors have preached on the dangers of individualism and narcissism. However, the influence of the two go far deeper than grist for sermons. Both individualism and narcissism infect our view of the Church. Let me explain what I mean.

In terms of individualism, many Church leaders assume that ministry must ultimately be defined in terms of the people in the Church as individuals. Our Gospel is most often preached to individuals. I doubt if many of us have preached in such a way so as to encourage an entire family to commit itself to Christ as was the case of the Philippian jailer. There are cultures in existence today where if one person makes a decision for Christ, the whole family, clan, or tribe must make the same decision. Some cultures naturally think in terms of the collective, whereas our culture thinks in terms of the individual. If the Church is a collection of individuals, then the mission of the Church will be defined accordingly.

In terms of narcissism, the underlying assumption of much of the leadership in the Church is that the Gospel has been given to meet the *needs*, even the *wants*, of the individual. How tragic! We have lost the vision that the Church exists to bring glory to God first, rather than to bring pleasure to His people. God may have a wonderful plan for our lives, but the greater question is whether or not sacrifice, taking up your cross, counting the cost, and denying father and mother can be thought of as wonderful in the contemporary sense of the word. In fact, the abundant life promised in Christ may bear little resemblance to the idyllic voyage promised by so many of us. Such a message may be functional in an age of individualism and narcissism, but is it Scriptural?

The problem with individualism and narcissism in terms of the Church's ministry to families lies in the relationship of the parts to the whole, a relationship of critical importance if we think in system terms. In any system the welfare of the whole outweighs the importance of the parts. In fact, the welfare of the parts is determined by the importance of the whole. The significance of the matter lies in the interrelationship between the two. The words of the apostle Paul echo through the corridors of Church history to remind us of the crucial importance of the whole, the part and the interrelationship between the two.

> For just as the body is one and has many members, and all the members of the body, though many, are one body, so it is with Christ. . . . But God has so composed the body, giving the greater honor to the inferior part, that there may be no discord in the body, but that the members may have the same care for one another. If one member suffers, all suffer together; if one member is honored, all rejoice together (I Cor. 12:12, 24-26, RSV).

If Paul is right, then one relevant issue for the Church is the relationship between the individual, the family, and the local church.

If we preach a gospel that neglects the welfare of the whole in exchange for the happiness of the individual, then the Church as a living, pulsing body is weakened as is the welfare of the family. We must recover the priority of interrelationship.

Chapter 3 suggested a model in which the interrelationship between the Church and the family is evaluated from the perspective of the whole. I suggested that a church can relate to the families of its members parasitically, competitively, cooperatively, or symbiotically. In that case I was arguing for the integrity of the family in terms of the integrity of the Church.

In this chapter I am arguing the same case but from a different perspective. In Chapter 3, I was concerned that the family not get lost in the Church's preoccupation with itself. The parts can be lost in the welfare of the whole. What I am arguing here is that we can also become so preoccupied with the individual that the family can get lost. The Church, as handmaiden to its culture, is in danger of that preoccupation. The individualism and narcissism of our personalized culture plays right into the individualism and narcissism of a church. The two can coexist. But the problem is that they cannot coexist in those terms and foster and strengthen family life at the same time. Individualism and narcissism on the part of either the person or a church mutually excludes a strong ministry to the families in that church. What does a healthy interrelationship between individual, family, and church look like if we use system terms?

You will remember that a system is defined as a cluster of highly interrelated parts, each responding to the other while at the same time maintaining itself as a whole. I am suggesting that the Church redefine itself in system terms as the whole but with the parts being *its families* rather than the individuals in those families. Even where there are no families, such as in the case of the single person or the between-families young adult, I am suggesting that the parts which make up the whole be construed as those clusters of primary relationships which function as family. The Church according to this redefinition becomes a family of families.

Again, current systems literature is helpful in teaching us how healthy systems function. In particular, two concepts surface in the description of healthy interrelationships. They are the concepts of adaptability and cohesion, which can be thought of as interacting with one another so as to form a model for evaluating family health. For purposes of our discussion I have adjusted the model to fit the evaluation of the Church in terms of its health where health is taken to mean a useful and mutually beneficial relationship between a church and its families.

Adaptability is taken to mean the ability of a system, in this case a church, to change its structure, including its power affiliations, its role definitions, and its relationship rules, in order to be responsive to situational and cultural stress. The assumption is that an adaptive system requires balancing both change and stability. A church, in order to be healthy, must be able to both promote change and support stability. If one is advanced at the expense of the other, then disease rather than health results.

Following this reasoning then, adaptability can be taken to extremes. At the one extreme is chaos where change takes place for the sake of change. Nothing is secure. Nothing is fixed. Everyone does what is right in his or her own eyes. At the other extreme is rigidity where change never takes place. What was once appropriate, forever remains in place. Structures become fixed and wooden even when their relevance is outmoded.

The two extremes breed their own problems. Chaos breeds faddishness, and rigidity breeds sterility. Neither facilitates health. Both facilitate the ultimate demise of the system.

At the center of the continuum is the quality of flexibility. A flexible system is one in which change is possible but stability is normal. If the environment changes, then so does the system. It possesses the ability to promote positive feedback, to know when and how to change. On the other hand, if the structures of the system are working, and if health is being promoted, then the presence of negative feedback informs the system to stay the way it is. Change is not needed. A healthy church is a flexible church.

The second concept is that of cohesion. According to systems literature, cohesion is the emotional bonding members have with one another and the relative degree of autonomy a person experiences in the system. What is of importance to us is the emphasis upon bonding and autonomy. When applied to the Church, it has to do with the relative degree of control a church has over its members versus the degree of autonomy from that church which is experienced by the family.

101

Like adaptability, cohesion can be taken to extremes. At the one extreme is dependency where the person, or in our model, the family, relies on the church for its sole source of support whether that reliance is in terms of spirituality, social contact, or emotional support. A church that is characterized by this kind of dependency is filled with families whose world is limited to the church. They are infants spiritually, socially, and emotionally. They are dependent upon the church almost for life itself.

At the other extreme from dependency is independence. Whereas dependency fosters total reliance on the church for existence, the independent church fosters a sense of autonomy among its families to such a degree that there is little or no sense of support or nurturance. The independent church becomes marked by rugged individualism and schism. It is a body with too many heads.

At the center of the continuum of cohesion is the balanced position of interdependency. Interdependency is that characteristic in which the families of the church have the capacity for independence but choose to put their sense of individualism aside for the sake of the body. Unity becomes more important than having one's own way. The giving and getting of nurturance and support are more important than the expression of one's own gifts, talents, and interests. It is a church marked by the fruit of the Spirit rather than only the gifts of the Spirit.

It is in the intersection of these two continua that we identify five interrelationship styles between the church and the family. Four are typical but operate at the extremes, and the fifth is our suggested model church. The figure on the following page demonstrates the relative positions of the five churches.

A brief word about the four churches that operate in the extreme, and then a further comment about the ideal.

Beginning at the upper left-hand quadrant is the Nomadic church. Such a church is chaotically dependent. By that I mean its relationship with its families is tenuous. They are dependent in that they are looking to the church to meet their spiritual, social, and emotional needs, but they are in a state of chaos. Perhaps it is a church filled with church shoppers. People moving from one church to another looking for the perfect "high," the place where their needs will be met completely. The families are like migrant workers moving from place to place depending on the season of the year or the prospects of the harvest. In this case the harvest is the ability of the person in the pulpit to entertain them or the ability of the church to keep them busy. It is a commuter church, a church of nomads.

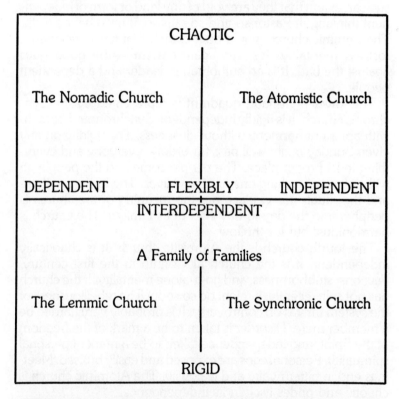

The church depicted at the lower left-hand quadrant of the model is what I have coined as the Lemmic church. A lemming is a small furry rodent known for its mass migrations in which hundreds of thousands throw themselves into the sea in the process of their migration. In our case it is the rigidly dependent church whose members blindly follow their leader or even one another to their own destruction. An example of the Lemmic church in the extreme would be the People's Temple of Jim Jones. The members of the church were rigidly bound to Jones and to one another even to the point of mass suicide. Though not as extreme, a Lemmic church might be one in which the peculiar teaching or charisma of the pastors or the tradition of the group dominates the thinking of the families in the church to such an extent that they are void of any kind or form of independent thinking. If Pastor so-and-so says so, it must be the truth. The Lemmic church would be a church that has developed a fortress mentality. It's "us against them"—the good guys against the bad. It is an authoritarian leader and a dependent people.

The lower right-hand quadrant is represented by the Synchronic church. It is rigidly independent. Synchronous has to do with apparent harmony without closeness. The rigidity on any given Sunday might well pass for order—everyone and everything in its proper place. The people come and the people go without ever touching one another's lives. The forms are there and the rituals are in place but the meaning of the church is peripheral to the day-to-day lives of its families. The church is harmonious, but it is hollow.

The fourth church is the Atomistic church. It is chaotically independent. It is the church at Corinth in the first century. Factions, stubbornness, and go-it-alone mentality. If the church has not split recently, it might do so soon. The rebelliousness of the system thrives on controversy. It is probably very hard to be a member there. Disorder is taken to be a mark of the freedom of the Spirit, and independence taken to be a mark of personal spirituality. Personal egos are exposed and easily bruised. Meetings end in bitter rivalry and jealously. The Atomistic church is chaotic and prides itself in its independence.

What I am suggesting is that a church that operates at any of the extremes is unhealthy in terms of its sense of interrelatedness. That some churches prosper at those extremes is only indicative of the nature of the times. The end result in every case will be dysfunction, perhaps not in the near future but ultimately. We always reap what we sow.

At the center of the model is the flexibly Interdependent

church. The families in this church have a healthy sense of belonging yet without feeling as if they are being possessed by the church. In fact, the church may well foster a sense of independence in the hope that its people will want rather than need to be there.

In a similar vein, the church fosters creativity and initiative. A sense of openness permeates the place. There is freedom without fear. There is a sense of the past as well as a sense of the present. God has been at work in the church in the past and is still at work in the church in the present. The presence of the Holy Spirit in their midst assures them of continuity without stagnation.

If you are a family in a flexibly Interdependent church you are aware of the support of others as well as the openness of others. Paradoxically there is a sense of permanence, not in the permanence of structures but in the permanence of friendship and commitment. The people are a people belonging to the Covenant God, and they belong as well to one another.

If what we know about health in family systems is true, then I am suggesting that the same holds true if the church envisions itself as a Family of Families. The members will feel a sense of belonging while at the same time experiencing a sense of freedom. Healthy families foster a sense of autonomy while at the same time fostering a sense of responsibility for one another. The whole is deemed necessary and important but never to the exclusion of the parts. In turn, the parts exhibit a sense of loyalty to the whole while becoming all that they can be. In an ideal sense the church is a place where the person, his or her family, and the church as a Family of Families thrive and prosper.

A New Role for the Pastor

It is one thing to suggest a new role for the church. It's another to make it happen. What's a pastor to do? Again, the same family systems literature that instructs us as to the health of family systems and the importance of adaptability and cohesion, also instructs us as to how this health is brought about. This time, however, we turn to the literature that deals with the family under stress. Much has been generated in the secular literature concerning the family under stress. What kind of family handles stress the best? The following is a compilation of patterns that I have extracted from the literature and have arranged into suggestions for the pastor of a Family of Families church. There are five dimensions of the pastoral role in terms of providing leadership for the church.

Promote Family Integration

First, the pastor of a Family of Families church must *promote a sense of family integration.* The term integration is used in the sense of bringing the parts together. A family that is well integrated has an attitude of "we're in this together." A church that exhibits this attitude has a sense of responsibility for one another. If something happens to one family in the church, it has happened to them all. No one is isolated.

For this to happen, the pastor must give something up in order to get something. What he must give up is his sense of being the primary care giver—his need to be needed. In terms of care giving he becomes one among many. What he gains is others who will share in the responsibility of care giving. He is not the only one whose duty it is to respond to others in need.

The other side of the issue of family integration is an attitude that "we do things together." A Family of Families church has a keen sense of fellowship. People like to be together, and the pastor fosters that kind of activity. Again, however, a slight change of orientation might be necessary. The change in orientation has to do with the division of activities into the secular and the sacred. Doing things together can be an end in itself. The sanctity of human work and play can be seen to be of value in and of itself. Whatever fosters the integration of the family and the church is good.

Encourage Family Adaptability

The second dimension of the pastor's role is the need to *encourage family adaptability.* We've already mentioned the

106

issue of adaptability so we need not expand on it too much here, except to add two additional thoughts. The first has to do with the need of the pastor to be personally flexible himself. He cannot expect his church to be adaptable if he isn't. The second has to do with the need of the church to be open and willing to change if needed. Such change can be either first-order or second-order change. First-order change is the kind of change that is allowed for by the existing rules and structures themselves. It is the easiest kind of change to initiate. Second-order change is more difficult because it requires thinking outside the lines. It involves the freedom to think in terms of new categories and in ways not tried before.

The difference between first-order and second-order change is what happens to me when I lose a golf ball on the golf course. My first-order solution is to look for it in the most obvious places. I look for it where it should have gone or in the same places I have found it before. Second-order change is to think outside the lines, to make myself think in terms of novel solutions. More often than not, second-order solutions work where first-order solutions fail.

Much of the history of the work of God in the world is a history of second-order solutions. God's choice of Israel was a second-order solution. Human wisdom would have never thought of choosing that nation. His choice of the Cross, like Israel, was indicative of second-order change. No one expected Him to send His Son as a substitute for us. That was unthinkable. Such is the nature of second- order change.

When it comes to the work of God in the world today, He is still in the business of second-order change. What is fascinating to me is the tendency of many of us to flock after a new and novel idea that has worked in someone else's church. A book is written about it, and we all are in the duplicating business. The problem is that if I always follow the example of someone else, I am always engaging in first-order thinking. The freedom of the Holy Spirit to be at work in my life and in the life of my church is inhibited by my resistance to second-order solutions. If I am a first-order thinker, the tendency will be for those families in my church to be first-order thinkers, too.

Facilitate Family Adjustment

The third dimension of the new role for the pastor is his need to *facilitate family adjustment*. Family adjustment has to do with fitting in with others. Secular research indicates that certain characteristics typify a family that is adjustable.

They are affectionate and sharing. They have the ability to be demonstrative and are unashamed of their feelings, both positive and negative.

They are vulnerable with one another. They risk sharing that part of themselves which constitutes their weaknesses and imperfections. They refuse to engage in phony shows of perfectionism, and they trust that others in the family will deal with them graciously just as they deal graciously.

Last of all, they are able to resolve their differences. Families that demonstrate adjustment are able to deal with each other assertively and not aggressively. They trust others to deal with them forthrightly and aboveboard. When there are hurt feelings, as there always are in healthy families, they are committed to working them through because the relationship is of more importance than being right or being hurt.

What is true of families is also true of a Family of Families. They are affectionate and sharing. They are vulnerable and equally committed to the constructive resolution of differences for the sake of unity and for the sake of the viability of relationships in the body.

Foster Individuation

The fourth dimension of the new role of the pastor is paradoxical. He needs to *foster individuation*. Rather than foster dependency, he must encourage his people to grow up in such a way so as not to need him. When families are strong in themselves, they are more likely to stay in a fellowship because they choose to rather than because they have no choice. Interdependency is a choice one makes to be in relationship with another. We can only make that choice if we have the option to be independent.

Develop Community

The fifth and last dimension of the new role for the pastor is his commitment to *develop a sense of community.* In this case, community is taken to be an all-inclusive term for what has been said above. At the heart of a sense of community is the incredibly important phenomenon of belonging. A church where community abounds is a church where its people belong as individuals and as families. Since the fall of Adam, mankind has wandered in a far country, wanting and needing to belong. Our first and most pressing need is to belong to God. That we can offer in Christ. But there is another need to belong. It is the need to be in meaningful relationship with others, to be in the I-Thou relationship rather than in the I-it relationship. It is the need to be bonded and healthily connected with others in the human family. Where better to find that relationship of community than in the church, a Family of Families?

What I am suggesting is old hat to many pastors. They can say with confidence that they have been doing most of this all along. Still, for others of us, it requires a facing of our own needs and fears as well as our own shortcomings. When you choose to be the shepherd of a Family of Families you must lay aside many of your own facades and elect to become a real and human person in your own right. You cannot afford to be less than real lest your flock be less than they can be. Granted, there are risks. However, whatever is good requires the taking of risks. Growth and development are not static terms. We should begin a steady and purposeful commitment to become family to one another so that the work of God in our lives might go forward and that His Kingdom be honored. The new role for the pastor is key in that growth and development.

A New Role for the Laity

Everything that I have said thus far is of significance to the layman. I would only add two other thoughts.

First, the laity needs to become "experts" in the area of family ministry. In Chapter 5, I briefly mentioned that a new responsibility falls on the shoulders of the Church. In the past we have abandoned the role of expert to those who have accumulated formal degrees. We have professionalized family ministry in the same way we have professionalized other ministry. If we stop and think, we will realize that the kind of skills that are important in leading others to maturity in family have little to do with formal education. What is important is personal experience, and that experience need not be one of total success. That is, I have something to say to others based upon my occasional failures as well as my successes. What is needed is for me to be open to others who come after me in terms of my own personal journey. Whether straight, smooth, rocky or crooked, I am a survivor. I have something to say based upon the experience I have gained and the wisdom I have gathered.

For those of us who must recruit others to serve with us in family ministry, I would remind us of the need to enlist as co-laborers those in our churches who have demonstrated a commitment to the issues we deem important. Our "experts" might be the most unlikely sort because they come to it quietly. These experts are the laymen in our churches who are recognized to be healthily in process. Their relationships give evidence of being whole and functional. If they are a husband and a wife, they can witness to the wholeness of their marriage. If they are parents, they can attest to relationships with their children that are full and meaningful. Whoever they are, they have come to their expertise in the school of hard knocks rather than in the classroom. If they have been exposed to formal education, all the better.

Theirs is a task of discipling, that of leading others to a place of health and wholeness as family people. The need of the Church is to find men and women who are willing to commit themselves to the task of family ministry at the level of personal and intimate involvement. It is a task that no other institution in modern society is fulfilling today. Because of that vacuum it is our greatest opportunity. It is a task for the laity.

The second thought in terms of a new role for the laity is the need to become extended family to one another. Our twentieth-century industrialized culture has lost touch with the meaning of the extended family. A brief illustration from my interaction with an African student is to the point. When we first met, I asked if he had brought his family with him from Africa. His answer was no. I responded by saying how lonely it must be for him to be here in the United States alone. He replied that he wasn't alone. I asked if he hadn't said that he had left his family in Africa? He replied that he wasn't lonely because his wife and children were with him in the States. I was confused. Then I realized the source of my misunderstanding. Family to him meant all of the brothers and sisters, the uncles and aunts, his mother and his father, cousins, and everybody else who were still in Africa—his clan.

The majority of families in the world outside the highly technological countries of the West consider family to be much broader than we do. Their concept of family includes the entire kinship network, where our concept usually includes only the closest of kin. The difficulty for us is the pressure that is placed upon the nuclear family when there is so little external support. If all there is is Mom, Dad, and the kids, then their relationships absorb a great deal of pressure. If there is a breakdown or severe dysfunction, to whom do they turn? For most of us there is nowhere to go.

If we are a Family of Families, however, there is someone to turn to. When there is loss, there is someone to fill the gap. When there is pain, there is someone to bring comfort. When there is irresponsibility, there is someone to confront. When there is ignorance, there is someone to show us what to do.

The Church as a Family of Families is a legitimate alternative to the loss of the extended family. What is needed is an openness to those relationships and an openness to God's working through us to others and His work in us through them. More than ever, as the contemporary gospel song says, "We really do need each other."

Conclusion

The concept of a Family of Families is at the heart of what this book is all about. In my opinion it is what the Church must be in

111

the last two decades of the twentieth century. The dreadful lack in the world today is in the area of meaningful and permanent relationships. The world is not only distant from God, it is also a conglomeration of people distant from one another. The alienation is pervasive.

It is true that the answer to the need of the world is the Gospel of God's grace in and through Jesus Christ. We cannot afford, however, to end the equation there. Jesus Christ is alive in the world today in the presence of His Church. His witness is our witness. Who we are He is. If we mirror the world in which we live in terms of our individualism and our narcissism, we bear false witness as to His nature. If we bear witness as to our love for one another and our belonging to one another, we mirror His true nature. The church of the first century was called to leave their earthly familial allegiances and to bond to one another as the new family of God. The revolutionary impact of the first-century church was their love for one another as Christ had commanded them. The need for the church in the twentieth century is to respond as they responded. We are the Church and we are family. Let us get on with our business.

9 We Face the Future Together

Future Shock is not just the title of a book. It is a reality. When it comes to ministry to families, the Church is caught between two mutually exclusive positions.

On the one hand we are committed to preserving the structures of the family as we know them. In the case of the Western industrial world those structures have taken the form of the nuclear family: Mom, Dad, and the kids.

On the other hand we are committed to ministering to the people of the world where they are. We recognize the futility of putting artificial barriers between them and the Gospel. The incarnation of Christ reminds us that God comes to us where we are, not where we ought to be. The structures of the family are changing in the world of today. A dilemma has been created. How can the dilemma be solved?

One answer has been to wear save-the-family buttons, to preach sermons, and to treat the issues as if they were simple. People are encouraged to retreat to another time in which the romantic ideals of the past were supposed to be a part of the fabric of everyday life. The problem with this approach is that there has never been a time when the ideals of the past have been reality. The family has always been in the process of change. It is the first institution that must adjust to the realities of life. What is often held out to be the golden mean, that is, the nuclear family intact and secure, has been the norm only for a few upper-class and upper-middle-class families during the last one or two hundred years. For most of human history women have worked outside the home in fields if not in offices. Dislocation in terms of famine and war have been the reality where now it is the mobility of job relocations and occupational migration. In much of the past, husbands didn't divorce their wives. They deserted them. There have always been single parent families. Our norms have been normal for a very select few.

The implication for the Church is rather subtle. By holding up the nuclear family as the irreplaceable norm, we artificially limit ourselves to a ministry to those who fit that norm. As the persons who fit those norms dwindle in number, more and more people fall outside the norms and thus outside the purview of ministry.

Those who are in the Church and do not fit the norms are made to feel as lepers, as if they really don't have a place.

I'm quite sure that those of us in positions of leadership do not intend for the ministry of the Church to be limited in this way. Nor do we want to be a part of the problem rather than a part of the solution. What are we to do?

Let's take a long, hard look at ourselves, our sermons, and our structures to see if they are flexible enough to adapt to the realities of the times, while at the same time holding fast to the truth of relationships as found in Scripture. What I am suggesting has a tension implicit in it. Such is the nature of change. You cannot afford to rest on your oars and still expect to get anywhere. What is therefore normal is a ministry characterized by openness to change with an evaluative process built into it. Such a ministry seeks God's wisdom as to what must be fixed and what can be flexible.

To stimulate that kind of dialogue, let me bring to you some of the realities of the future in terms of the family of the future and the future of the family.

The Family of the Future

Over the last several years the one person who seems to have had the best grasp on the realities of the changing American family is Paul C. Glick, Senior Demographer at the U.S. Bureau of the Census. His predictions of the cast and shape of things to come has been uncanny. No one in American academia has influenced the direction of thinking about the changing nature of the family more than has Glick. In late 1979 he wrote an article entitled "Future American Families," stating what he thought to be the direction of the American family through the 1980's. The article and its provocative conclusions give the Church much to think about. Based upon his thinking and others, I would like to suggest seven trends concerning the family of the future and their implications for the Church.

1. Change will come slower.
According to Glick three factors underlie what he predicts to

be a slowdown in the rate of change as it is taking place within the family. The first has to do with the birthrate. The U.S. birthrate reached its peak about two decades ago, and much of the momentum for change during those decades has come from that increased rate. Communities built schools to educate the children. Churches built educational buildings to cope with increased numbers. But the birthrate has been declining for the last 20 years, and the experts expect it to remain about the same during the next 20.

The second factor that will slow the rate of change is related to the first. The great increase in college enrollments during the last 20 years is unlikely to be repeated again in the next couple decades. Thus the Church will cease to be as "young" as it once was. The portent for church-related higher education is significant.

And thirdly, the proportion of women in the labor force which increased from 38 percent in 1960 to 50 percent in 1978 will increase more slowly to only about 57 percent in 1995. More moms are working than before, and they will continue to work but not in such rapidly increasing numbers as before. In addition to the impact upon the family, the working woman impacts the Church as well. Gone are the days of cheap volunteer labor to handle anything from Daily Vacation Bible School to work in the church office. Most of the women who are at home either have very young children, are older, or have an income level which allows them the freedom not to work.

All three factors coalesce to slow the rate in which change has been thrust upon the family and thus upon the Church.

2. There will be more singles.

Two factors seem to account for this trend.

First of all, young adults in the United States are postponing marriage. This has resulted from what demographers have labeled the marriage squeeze, the varying proportion of males to females in the marriageable age range. In the early 1980's the squeeze is in terms of marriageable men to women. There will be more women than men. However, by the middle 1980's that trend will reverse itself, and there will be more men than women. The greater factor has to do with what happens when men or women postpone marriage to a later date: the longer they postpone marriage, the more likely they are to remain unmarried throughout life. Hence, instead of four to five percent never marrying as in the recent past, eight to nine percent of young adults now in their twenties may experience a lifetime of singlehood. According to Glick that represents a percentage last reached during the Great Depression of the 1930s.

The second factor has to do with the issue of divorce. The divorce rate for married women doubled from 10.6 per 1,000 in 1965 to 20.3 per 1,000 in 1975. Since 1975 the rate has increased but at a slower rate—22.0 per 1,000 married women in 1978. Although the rate has slowed, the percentage in terms of age range has changed. Earlier on, the highest frequency for divorce was in the younger than 25 category. Now the range seems to be moving upward. Glick predicts that the greatest proportion of divorces in the 1980's may hit the 25- to 39-year-olds. The high rate of divorce will remain the same but the divorceé population will be older. And it is known that the older people are when they divorce, the less likely they will be to remarry.

What does this mean for the Church? It means that there will be more singles, both never married and formerly married, and they will tend to be older. It also means that the Church will be pressed to look again at its Scriptural positions regarding divorce and remarriage. The sheer numbers will demand a reevaluation.

3. The problem of POSSLQ

1980 marked the first time the U.S. Bureau of the Census included a category on their census forms which counted "People of Opposite Sex Sharing Living Quarters." POSSLQ. The numbers are staggering. In 1970 the Census Bureau estimated that approximately 530,000 couples (or 1.1 million adults of the opposite sex) were unmarried but living together. In 1978 that number had doubled to 1,130,000 couples (or 2.3 million adults). What is even more amazing is the estimate that the proportion increased 19 percent from 1977 to 1978. If the numbers continue to increase as they have in the past, there will be as many young unmarried couples living together as there are married. What will the Church do?

Our tendency has been to exclude them because they have broken our rules. If we take this position, they will automatically stay beyond our influence. If, on the other hand, we take them in, no questions asked, we dilute our moral standards, and we weaken the integrity of marriage.

Frankly, I don't have a complete answer. I'm certainly not advocating a "Young Unmarried Couples Class" in our churches, nor am I advocating a carte blanche approach to their inclusion. What I do suggest is that we realize that many young couples live together rather than marry because they have been traumatized by earlier relationships, often as observed in their families of origin. They live together unmarried because they lack the quality of hope and because they are infected with the quality of impermanence. What the Church must have is open doors. Again, I remind you that Christ comes to us where we are and not where we ought to be. I would think that the Church must, therefore, be inclusive while at the same time prophetic. The Gospel is for sinners most of all. The Church must remember that, we are all in sin. At the same time we must give witness to the Gospel that dispels hopelessness and provides a caring community where permanence is the norm. Sinlessness is not a criterion for membership in the Body of Christ. A faith relationship with Christ is. What is of greater importance is the direction the person is traveling since having received Christ. Repentance, turning to God from idols, marks the beginning not the end of a process. The bottom line I would think is the need for the Church and its eldership to consider each unmarried, living-together couple who comes to it, one at a time. I suggest that we say two things: you are welcome and have a home here, but you must be open to the witness of the Spirit in your lives as to your living conditions. Sooner or later every church will face the problem of POSSLQ.

4. There will be more one-parent families.
    In 1978 the Census Bureau figures indicate that 19 percent or

117

the 63 million children in America (excluding those living in institutions) were living in a one-parent family. Though large, that figure is deceiving. Most children who are living with one-parent are in a transition between two successive two-parent families. According to Paul Glick, "By 1990 probably more than one-half of all children will have spent some of the time before they reach 18 years of age in a one-parent family or household."

The implications for the Church are as staggering as are the numbers. We must remember that often a one-parent family is a hurting family. Divorce and death tear the survivors to pieces. Finances are skewed and the energy of the remaining adult is drained. Both the children and the remaining parent need support. Both need their church to be the Church. We cannot allow 50 percent of our children to spend any part of their years in the isolation of a between-the-lines family. Human beings do not survive well when caught between the parentheses. It is a time for second-order thinking. We must become a Family of Families.

5. The time for child bearing will be shortened.

In the early years of the twentieth century the average family consisted of four children and their parents. In the 1930's the average number of children decreased to three. The numbers have been falling until the present time where the family forming in the 1980's can expect to have two children on the average. The natural result is that couples spend less of their lives having and raising children. Therefore, young couples who remain married can expect to live as a child-free twosome for about 14 years longer than previous generations. In terms of the Church's family ministry, the need for an emphasis upon marriage enrichment increases the more couples focus on their marriage. It's far easier to focus on your marriage when your children are older and even easier when they are grown and gone.

6. There will be longer "empty nests."

This trend is the natural corollary of the preceding one.

Because couples have smaller families they can be expected to launch their children when they are at a younger age. In the past, couples had babies well into their thirties. Now they tend to stop in their middle to later twenties. It is not uncommon for a woman to have completed her child-rearing functions and responsibilities when she is in her early forties. This trend coupled with the trend for more women to be in the out-of-home work force, suggests the need for the Church to become more actively supportive of dual career families. It also suggests a greater need for freedom on the part of those in the empty-nest stage. The demands for flexibility on the part of the Church must be recognized. We must find a way to coexist in peace.

7. There will be more older adults.

This trend has been well documented and commented on in the literature. I only mention it here to reinforce the need of the Church to speak more directly to the needs of older married persons and to the needs of those who have been widowed. Every increase in life expectancy brings mammoth implications for the Church in terms of "widows who are widows indeed." The Church cannot ignore its direct and explicit command to care for those who have become needy and destitute. The increase in the number of older adults is both a responsibility and a privilege. As such, it is a growing opportunity for ministry.

The family of the future may well be somewhat unlike the family of the past. The task for the Church is to be open to God and to be willing to engage in creative ministry. The family is changing, and change is often hard. But we must remember that it has been in times of change that God has brought about much in the way of good. We need not fear the future.

The Future of the Family

I am optimistic about the future of the family. As you can tell from the tone of this book, I reject a doomsday approach while at the same time I trumpet the need for the Church to be doing far more than it is now doing. The truth of the matter is that families of one form or another will continue. There will always be families. What may not continue is the romantic ideal of the intact nuclear family as the norm. The task of socialization will always be needed as will the need for procreation. Our culture will not kill itself off except in the unthinkable case of a nuclear war. All things considered, we can be bullish about the family.

What makes me even more optimistic is the growing awareness in the Church that it must do more than it is now doing. If the past has accomplished one thing, it has gotten our attention. We all know something must be done. The trick will be in the doing of it.

Though I am optimistic, I am concerned, and my concern can be expressed as two reminders:

First, the mission of the Church is to make disciples for Jesus Christ. In the recent past that task has been accomplished in the main by the local expression of the Body of Christ, the local church. An entire superstructure has grown up in support of that local congregation. Denominations, world councils, associations, all exist for the ultimate purpose of strengthening that local body.

The local body, however, has come to mean the local place rather than the local people in the minds of some. What I would remind you is that when it comes to people, they first of all and most naturally come wrapped up in families. The task of the Church is to support and encourage those most primal units. When they do their job well and are trained to disciple their own, they do it best. The job of the Church is not to take the place of the family. It is to encourage the family to be all that God intends it to be.

I have suggested that the best way this task can be furthered is for each church to become a Family of Families. We are to enter into our task together, not as competitors, but as colaborers. We, the Church and the family, are about the same thing in terms of God's will for us. Family ministry is, therefore, not an option. It is a necessity.

Second, if you will remember, I suggested that our culture is infected with a twofold blight: individualism and narcissism. I also suggested that the Church can become infected with the same blight but in different ways. The Church can become a place where the individual is held up to be the end result of all ministry and the happiness and wholeness of that individual the end result of all programs.

If this is true, we face a real problem. It is the problem of consumerism. It is the good old American way for the consumer to set the standards for his or her own consumption. The Neilson ratings measure what the average Amercian family watches on TV, and we are flooded with inane sitcoms and game shows. The consumer is king.

The consumer says through market research that he or she wants tight jeans so we are bombarded with tight pants and suggestive adds. The consumer is king.

The consumer supports pornography on cable TV so an increasing number of neighborhoods in America have X-rated movies available at the flick of a switch. The consumer is king.

If the consumer is king in the Church, then the Church will settle for the lowest common denominator and the most popular church becomes the best church. That cannot be right.

In the Church, God is to be King and His Kingdom is to be first. We are not in a popularity contest with the world. The prophetic mission of the Church is to challenge the spirit of the age, to do what is right and what is best, not necessarily what the majority wants.

I cannot believe that it is God's will that either the Church or the family is meant to live a diseased and tragic life. God intends for us both to prosper, not in the materialistic or narcissistic sense of the word but in the eschatological sense of the word. God intends for us to be a part of the working out of His will for the Church in human history. The *eschaton* is that purpose of God toward which history is moving and in which we all will find our greatest meaning. It is the Church *and* the family together doing the work and the will of God. "United we stand; divided we fall" was true for our country in another traumatic day and age, and it is true here and now for the Church and the family.

SELECTED BIBLIOGRAPHY—Chapter 1

BARTH, K. *Church Dogmatics,* Vol. III, part 2. Edinburgh: T. & T. Clark, 1956.
BONHOEFFER, D. *Letters and Papers from Prison.* New York: Macmillan, 1971.
BRUNNER, E. *The Theology of Emil Brunner,* Charles Kegley. New York: Macmillan, 1962.

SELECTED BIBLIOGRAPHY—Chapter 2

BARTH, K. *Church Dogmatics,* Vol. III, part 2. Edinburgh: T. & T. Clark, 1956.
BECKER, H. *Outsiders: Studies in the Sociology of Deviance.* New York: The Free Press, 1963.
BERKOUWER, G. *Man: The Image of God.* Grand Rapids, Mich.: Eerdmans, 1962.
BONHOEFFER, D. *Letters and Papers from Prison.* New York: Macmillan, 1971.
BRIM, ORVILLE. *Socialization After Childhood.* New York: John Wiley, 1966.
BROWN, R. *A First Language.* Cambridge: Harvard University Press, 1973.
BRUNNER, E. *The Theology of Emil Brunner,* Charles Kegley. New York: Macmillan, 1962.
COOLEY, CHARLES. *Human Nature and the Social Order.* New York: Charles Scribner's Sons, 1922.
COOLEY, CHARLES. *Social Organization.* New York: Charles Scribner's Sons, 1929.
DeFLEUR, M., W. D'ANTONIO, and S. DeFLEUR. *Sociology: Man in Society.* Glenview, Ill.: Scott, Foresman and Co., 1971.
GIBBS, J. "Conceptions of Deviant Behavior," *Pacific Sociological Review,* Vol. 9, Spring, 1966.
GOLDBERG, S. and F. DEUTSCH. *Life-Span Individual and Family Development.* Monterey, Calif.: Brooks/Cole Publishing Co., 1977.
GOSLIN, D. *Handbook of Socialization Theory and Research.* Chicago: Rand McNally, 1969.
HARLOW, H. and M. HARLOW. "Learning to Love," *American Scientist,* 1966, 54 (3) 244-272.
JONES, E. and H. GERARD. *Foundations of Social Psychology.* New York: John Wiley and Sons, 1967.
LADD, G. *A Theology of the New Testament.* Grand Rapids, Mich.: Eerdmans, 1974.
LINDSMITH, A. and A. STRAUSS. *Social Psychology.* New York: Holt, Rinehart and Winston, 1968.
LYNN, D. *The Father: His Role in Child Development.* Monterey, Calif.: Brooks/Cole Publishing Co., 1974.
MEAD, G. *Mind, Self and Society.* Chicago: University of Chicago Press, 1934.
MUSSEN, P., J. COUGER, J. KAGAN and J. GEIWITZ. *Psychological Development: A Life Span Approach.* New York: Harper and Row, 1979.
OEPKE. "Baptidzo" (Baptism) in Kittel, G., *Theological Dictionary of the New Testament,* Vol. 1. Grand Rapids, Mich.: Eerdmans, 1964.
PARSONS, T. and R. BALES. *Family Socialization and Interaction Process.* New York: The Free Press, 1955.
RENGSTORF. "Mathetas," (disciple) in Kittel G., *Theological Dictionary of the New Testament,* Vol. IV. Grand Rapids, Mich.: Eerdmans, 1967.
SAGER, CLIFFORD. *Marriage Contracts and Couple Therapy.* New York: Brunner/Mazel, 1976.
SCHWARTZ, R. and J. SKOLNICK. "Two Studies of Legal Stigma," in Becker, H. *Outsiders: Studies in the Sociology of Deviance.* New York: The Free Press, 1963.

SULLIVAN, H. *The Interpersonal Theory of Psychiatry.* New York: W.W. Norton and Co., 1953.
TURNER, RALPH. *Family Interaction.* New York: John Wiley and Sons, 1970.

SELECTED BIBLIOGRAPHY—Chapter 6

BOULDING, K. E. "General Systems Theory—The Skeleton of Science," *General Systems,* L. Von Bertalanffy, editor (1956), 1, 11-17.
BRODY, W. M. "A Cybernetic Approach to Family Therapy," *Family Therapy and Disturbed Families,* G. H. Zeek and I. Boxzormenyi-Nagy, editors. Palo Alto, Calif.: Science and Behavior Books, Inc., 1967.
BUCKLEY, W. *Sociology and Modern Systems Theory.* Englewood Cliffs, N.J.: Prentice-Hall, 1967.
BUCKLEY, W., editor. *Modern Systems Research for the Behavioral Scientist.* Chicago: Aldine Publishing Co., 1968.
HALL, A. D. and R. E. FAGEN. "Definition of a System," *General Systems* (1956) 1, 18-28.
KANTOR, DAVID, and WILLIAM LEHR. *Inside the Family: Toward a Theory of Family Process,* San Francisco: Jossey-Bass, Inc., 1975.
SPEER, D. C. "Family Systems: Morphostasis and Morphogenesis, or 'Is Homeostasis Enough?' " *Family Process* (1970), 9, 259-278.
VON BERTALANFFY, L. "General Systems Theory—A Critical Review," *General Systems* (1962), 7, 1-20.
VON BERTALANFFY, L. *General Systems Theory* (revised edition). New York: George Braziller, 1968.

SELECTED BIBLIOGRAPHY—Chapter 7

EDDINGTON, SIR ARTHUR. *The Nature of the Physical World.* Ann Arbor: University of Michigan Press, 1958.
KANTOR, DAVID, and WILLIAM LEHR. *Inside the Family: Toward a Theory of Family Process,* San Francisco: Jossey-Bass, Inc., 1975.
MARUYAMA, M. "The Second Cybernetics: Deviation-Amplifying Mutual Causal Processes," *Modern Systems Research for the Behavioral Scientist,* W. Buckley, editor. Chicago: Aldine, 1968.

SELECTED BIBLIOGRAPHY—Chapter 8

HILL, R. *Families Under Stress.* New York: Harper and Brothers, 1949.
OLSON, D. H., et al. "Circumplex Model of Marital and Family Systems," *Family Process,* Vol. 18, I, April 1979.

SELECTED BIBLIOGRAPHY—Chapter 9

GLICK, P. C. "Future American Families," *The C.O.F.O. Memo,* Vol. II, No. 3.

	DATE DUE		